TRAVELS IN BAKUMATSU JAPAN

Published by TOYO PRess:

TOYO REFERENCE SERIES
Isabella Lucy Bird, *Traveling Japan's Deep Interior*
John la Farge, *An Artist in Japan*
Lafcadio Hearn, *Hearn's Japan. Vols. I-XIV*
Aimé Humbert, *Bakumatsu Japan*
Lucian Swift Kirtland, *Samurai Trails*
Ernest Satow, *Japan's Critical Years*
Marie Stopes, *A Japanese Journal*

TOYO ILLUSTRATED EDITIONS
Eiko Ozaki, *Warriors of Old Japan*
Lafcadio Hearn, *Hearn's Japan*

TRAVELS IN BAKUMATSU JAPAN

ROBERT FORTUNE

EDITED BY WILLIAM DE LANGE

TOYO REFERENCE SERIES

Contents

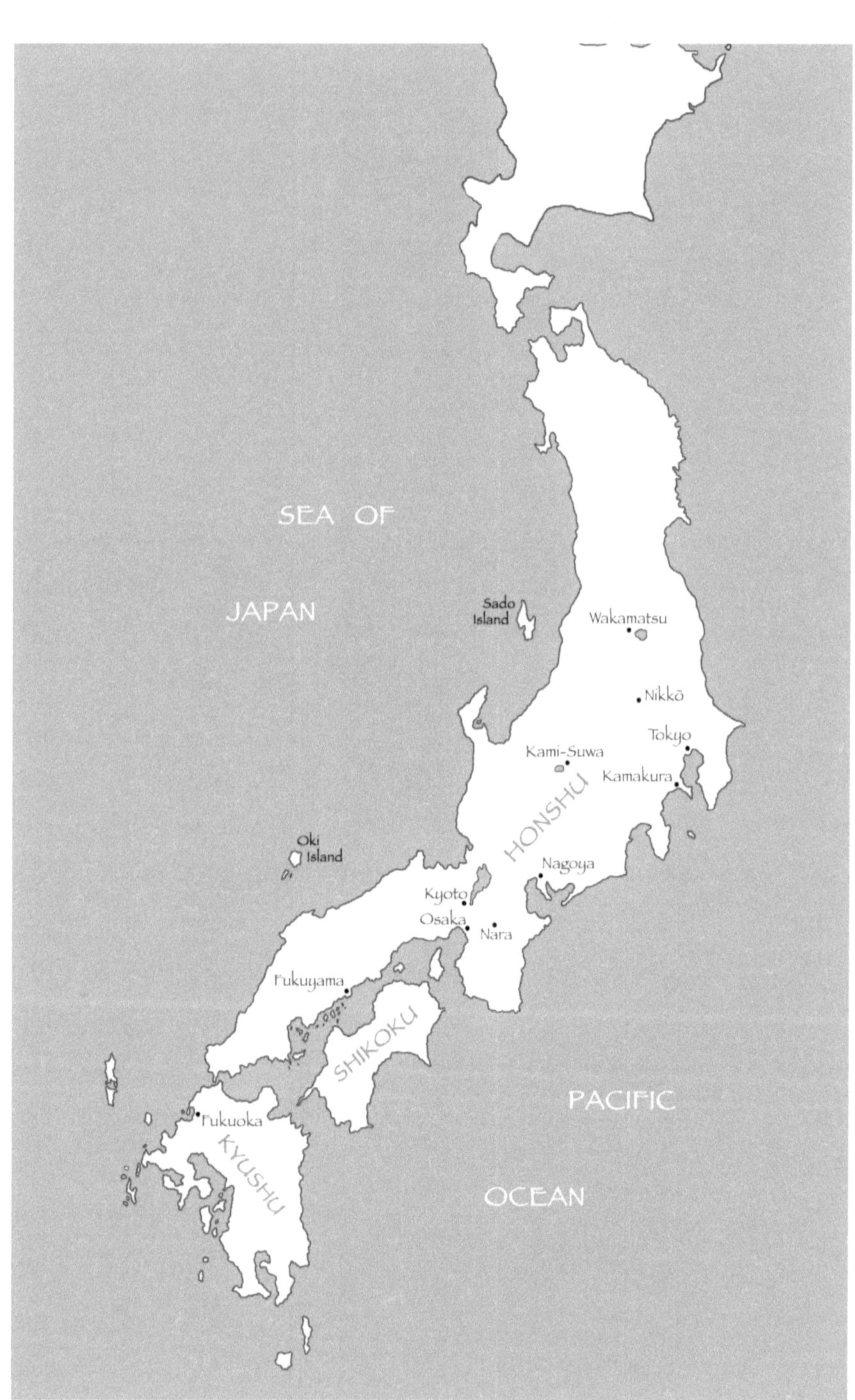

SEA OF
JAPAN
Sado
Island
Wakamatsu
Nikkō
Tokyo
Kami-Suwa
Kamakura
HONSHU
Oki
Island
Nagoya
Kyoto
Osaka
Nara
Fukuyama
SHIKOKU
PACIFIC
Fukuoka
KYUSHU
OCEAN

Nagasaki

At daylight on the 12th of October, 1860, the swift little barque *Marmora*, in which I was a passenger from China, was rapidly approaching the coast of Japan—a country at the ends of the earth, and well named by its inhabitants "the Kingdom of the Origin of the Sun." When I came on deck in the morning the far-famed shores of Zipangu lay spread before my wondering eyes for the first time. Having heard and read so many stories of this strange land—of its stormy coasts, on which many a goodly vessel had been wrecked; of its fearful earthquakes, which were said to have thrown up, in a single night, mountains many thousands of feet above the level of the sea; of its luxuriant vegetation, full of strange and beautiful forms; of its curious inhabitants; and last, but not least, of its salamanders!—I had long looked upon Japan much in the same light as the Romans regarded our own isles in the days of the ancient Britons.

My first view of these shores did a good deal towards dispelling this delusion. It was a lovely morning. The sun rose from behind the eastern mountains without a cloud to obscure his rays. The Gotō islands and Cape Ose were passed to the north of us, and with a fair wind and smooth sea we were rapidly approaching the large island of Kyushu, on which the town of Nagasaki is situated. The land is hilly and mountainous, and in many instances it rises perpendicularly from the sea. These perpendicular rocky cliffs have a very curious appearance as one sails along. There are also a number of queer-looking detached little islands dotted about; and one almost wonders how they got there, as they seem to have no connexion with any other land near them. Some of them are crowned with a scraggy pine tree or two, and look exactly like those bits of rockwork in the gardens of China and Japan. No doubt these rocky islands have suggested the idea worked out in gardens, and they have been well imitated. Others of these rocks look in the distance like ships under full sail, and in one instance I observed a pair of them exactly like fishing junks, which are generally met with in pairs. Nearer the shore the islands are richly clothed with trees and brushwood, resembling those pretty "Pulos" of the Eastern Archipelago. The highest hills on this part of the mainland of Kyushu are about 1500 feet above sea level; but hills of every height, from 300 to 1500 feet, and of all forms, were exposed to our view as we approached the entrance to the harbour of Nagasaki. Many of these hills were terraced nearly to their summits, and at this season these terraces were green with the young crops of wheat and barley.

The pretty little island of Papenberg (Takaboko-*jima*) stands as if it were a sentinel guarding the harbour of Nagasaki. Pretty it certainly is, and yet it is associated with scenes of persecution, cruelty, and bloodshed of the most horrible description. "If history spoke true," says Captain Sherard Osborn, "deeds horrid enough for it to have been for ever blighted by God's wrath have been perpetrated there during the persecutions of the Christians in the seventeenth century." It was the Golgotha of the many martyrs to the Roman Catholic faith. There by day and by night its steep cliffs had rung with the agonized shrieks of strong men or the wail of women and children launched to rest after torture in the deep waters around the island. If Jesuit records are to be believed, the fortitude and virtue exhibited by their Japanese converts in those sad hours of affliction have not been excelled in any part of the world since religion gave another plea to man to destroy his fellow creature. May it not be that the beauty with which nature now adorns that rock of sorrows is her halo of glory around a spot rendered holy by the sufferings of many that were brave and good.

As we passed the island we gazed with awe and pity on its perpendicular side from which these Christians were cast headlong into the sea. As soon as our ship rounded Papenberg the harbour and town of Nagasaki came full into view. On each side of this entrance to the bay there are numerous batteries apparently full of guns. On Papenberg itself, as well as on every little island and headland, fortifications were observed as we sailed along. There is also a flagstaff and telegraph station on one of the hills and the moment a ship is seen approaching a signal is made and passed on to Nagasaki. We were not molested by either guard boat or customhouse officer but allowed to sail quietly in to our anchorage. Here we were boarded by sundry officials who immediately began to put all sorts of questions regarding the ship her cargo and passengers and the information obtained was all committed to paper. The commanding officer was then informed that two of these gentry would be left on board and he was requested to give them shelter and accommodation in the cabin.

The harbour of Nagasaki is one of the most beautiful in the world. It is about a mile in width and three or four in length. When you are inside it appears to be completely landlocked and has all the appearance of an inland lake. The hills around it are some 1500 feet in height and their surface is divided and broken up by long ridges and deep glens or valleys that extend far up towards the summits. These ridges and glens are for the most part richly wooded while all the more fertile spots are terraced and under cultivation. The whole scene presents a quiet and charming picture of nature's handiwork intermingled with the labor of man. On the south side of the harbour there has been a portion of land set apart for the subjects of foreign nations whose governments have lately made treaties with Japan. The various consuls, most of whom are also merchants, reside at present in small houses or temples on the sides of the hill behind the settlement It is an interesting sight to see the flags of several Western nations, English, French, American and Portuguese—flying at this distance from home. A great portion of the land set apart for the foreign settlement was in the course of being reclaimed from the sea, and ere long a town of considerable size will rise on the shores of this beautiful bay.

The island of Deshima—dear old Deshima, where the Dutch have traded and dreamed so long—lies a little further up the bay, and looks in the distance like a small fort or breastwork, which is about 600 feet in length, and 240 in width. In these days, when Japan has to a great extent been opened to foreigners, it is amusing to read the account of the restrictions placed upon the movements of the Dutch during the period when all the trade of Japan was their own. The little island was only separated from Nagasaki by a narrow canal spanned by a stone bridge, but the dwellers on either side were prevented from seeing each other by means of a high wall. The bridge was closed by a gate, beside which was a guardhouse occupied by police and soldiers; and no one was allowed to quit the island on any pretense without the permission of the governor. Japanese were not allowed to visit the Dutch without permission, excepting those who were appointed to inspect their dwelling place, and then only at certain hours. The Japanese servants of the Dutch Factory were obliged to leave the island at sunset, and to report themselves at the guardhouse to prove that they had really left the Factory. The only individuals exempt from leaving the island at sunset were women who had forfeited the first claim of their sex to respect or esteem, and no female of good character was permitted on any pretense to set foot on Deshima. A placard set up near the bridge gate announced this in the plainest and coarsest terms.

When any member of the Factory wished to visit the town of Nagasaki, or the country in its vicinity for a little recreation or amusement, he was obliged to send in a petition to the governor twenty-four hours beforehand. Leave was usually granted, provided the captive was accompanied by a certain number of officials, police officers, and a compradore. These again had their servants and friends, so that the attendants and hangers-on of one unfortunate pleasure-seeker usually amounted to some twenty or thirty persons, all of whom he was bound to entertain.

On entering the town of Nagasaki the pleasure party was soon surrounded and followed by all the boys and idlers within reach, who shouted "*Holanda! Holanda!*" or "*Holanda Capitan!*" in the Dutchman's ears, and rendered his walk anything but an agreeable one. The excursion into the surrounding country must, however, have fully repaid the unfortunate captive for the disagreeables of the town. The scenery amongst the hills is of the most charming description, and must have been fully appreciated by men who were cooped up on a little mud-bank like the island of Deshima.

Such was the state of affairs only three or four years ago. At the time of my visit in the autumn of 1860 all this had undergone a wonderful change—certainly wonderful for Japan. The old bridge that connects the island with the town of Nagasaki is still there, and presents a venerable and somewhat ruinous aspect; the guardhouse is now empty, the gate has been removed, a part of the wall has been thrown down, and the Dutch are no longer the prisoners they once were. Like other foreigners, they can now visit the town when they choose, and roam about the surrounding country to any distance within twenty-five or thirty miles, without any interference from the Japanese.

In my wanderings in Deshima I stumbled upon a large rough piece of rock, on which were carved the words "Kaempfer" and "Thunberg." No other eulogy was necessary. It is pleasing to note that the modern Dutch revere the names of these men of science who have done so much to make us acquainted with the people and natural productions of Japan.

Opposite Deshima, and on the other side of the bay, the Japanese have a large factory in active operation. The machinery has been imported from Europe, and the superintendents are Dutch. The Japanese workmen appear to be most expert hands at molding, casting, and in the general management of steam machinery. In this respect they are far in advance of their neighbors the Chinese. Indeed, to adopt everything foreign they find useful, however different it may be from what they possess themselves, and to make themselves masters of the mode of working it, is a marked feature in the character of the Japanese people.

Nagasaki is situated on the northern shores of the bay, and is supposed to contain about 70,000 inhabitants. It is about a mile in length, and three-quarters of a mile in width, and fills up the space of ground between the shores of the bay and the hills that surround it. The streets are wide and clean compared with those in Chinese towns; but as a general rule the shops are poor, and contain few articles of much value. Substances used as food, eggshell porcelain, lacquerware of an inferior kind, and modern bronzes, are plentiful and comparatively cheap. Although the houses of the common people have a poor and mean appearance, there are some of considerable pretensions. Curiously enough, the largest and most notable buildings in the town, if we except the palace of the governor, are what are called tea-houses—places of amusement, where the entertainments are not such as accord with our ideas of morality. They seem at the present day much in the same condition in which Engelbert Kaempfer found them nearly two hundred years ago.

> The handsomest buildings, belonging to the townspeople, are two streets all occupied by courtesans. The girls in these establishments, which abound throughout Japan, are purchased of their parents when very young. The price varies in proportion to their beauty and the

number of years agreed for, which is, generally speaking, ten or twenty, more or less. They are very commodiously lodged in handsome apartments, and great care is taken to teach them to dance, sing, play upon musical instruments, to write letters, and in all other respects to make them as agreeable as possible. The older ones instruct the young ones, and these in their turn serve the older ones as their waiting maids. Those who make considerable improvement, and for their beauty and agreeable behavior are oftener sent for, to the great advantage of their masters, are also better accommodated in clothes and lodging, all at the expense of their lovers, who must pay so much the dearer for their favors. One of the sorriest must watch the house overnight, in a small room near the door, free to all comers upon the payment of one *mase*. Others are sentenced to keep the watch by way of punishment for their misbehavior.

After having served their time, if they are married, they pass among the common people for honest women, the guilt of their past lives being by no means laid to their charge, but to that of their parents or relations, who sold them in their infancy for so scandalous a way of getting a livelihood, before they were able to choose a more honest one. Besides, as they are generally well bred, that makes it less difficult for them to get husbands. The keepers of these houses, on the contrary, though possessed of never so plentiful estates, are for ever denied admittance into honest company.

The houses of the high officials, wealthy merchants, or retired gentlemen, though generally small, and only of one or two stories in height, are comfortable and cleanly dwelling places. One marked feature of the people, both high and low, is a love for flowers. Almost every house with any pretension to respectability has a flower garden in the rear, oftentimes indeed small, but neatly arranged; this adds greatly to the comfort and happiness of the family. As the lower parts of the Japanese houses and shops are open both before and behind, I had peeps of these pretty little gardens as I passed along the streets; and wherever I observed one better than the rest I did not fail to pay it a visit. Everywhere the inhabitants received me most politely, and permitted me to examine their pet flowers and dwarf trees. Many of these places are exceedingly small, some not much larger than a good-sized dining room; but the surface is rendered varied and pleasing by means of little mounds of turf, on which are planted dwarf trees kept clipped into fancy forms, and by miniature lakes, in which gold and silver fish and tortoises disport themselves. It is quite refreshing to the eye to look out from the houses upon these gardens. The plants generally seen in them were the following—*Cycas revoluta Azaleas*, the pretty little dwarf variegated bamboo introduced by me into England from China, Pines, Junipers, Taxus, *Podocarpus, Rhapis Flabelliformis*, and some ferns. These gardens may be called the gardens of the respectable working classes.

Japanese gentlemen in Nagasaki, whose wealth enables them to follow out their favorite pursuits more extensively, have another class of gardens. These, although small according to our ideas, are still considerably larger than those of the working classes; many of them are about a quarter of an acre in extent. They are generally turfed over; and, like the smaller ones, they are laid out with an undulating surface, some parts being formed into little mounds, while others are converted into lakes. In several of these places I met with azaleas of extraordinary size—much larger than I have ever seen in China, or in any other part of the world, the London exhibitions not excepted. One I measured was no less than 40 feet in circumference! These plants are kept neatly nipped and clipped into a fine round form, perfectly flat on the top, and look like dining room tables. They must be gorgeous objects when in flower. *Farfugium graiide* and I found many other variegated plants still undescribed in these gardens, in addition to those I have named as being favorites with the lower orders.

One old gentleman to whom I was introduced by my friend Mackenzie—Matotsuki—has a nice collection of pot plants arranged on stages, much in the same way as we arrange them in our greenhouses in England. Amongst them I noted small plants of the beautiful *Sciadopitys verticillata*, several *Setinosporas*, some with variegated leaves; *Thujopsis dolabrata*, and variegated examples of laurel, bamboo, orontium, and *Hoya Matotsukii*—a name given by some Dutch botanist in honor of the old gentleman, and of which he was not a little proud. Matotsuki is a fine mild-looking Japanese, rather beyond middle age. He has a collection of birds, such as gold and silver pheasants; and in his library are some illustrated botanical books, which he shows with great pride to his visitors. He presented me with a few rare plants from his collection, and offered to procure me some others, of which he had no duplicates in his own garden.

In the course of my rambles I came upon some tubs containing living salamanders for sale, and in the same quarter I observed some striking and beautiful kinds of fowls. These were rather above the ordinary size, but were remarkable for their fine plumage. The tail-feathers were long and gracefully curved, and fine silky ones hung down on each side of the hinder part of the back. Bantams were also plentiful, and bold independent-looking little fellows they appeared to be.

Three streams of water, spanned by numerous bridges, run down from the hills through the town; but at the time of my visit they were nearly dry. Besides supplying the town with water, they are used in summer for purposes of irrigation, and for driving water mills.

A Chinese town of this size and importance would have had walls and fortifications, but there is nothing of the kind at Nagasaki. Indeed, such a mode of defense does not seem to be common in Japan. The streets have gates thrown across them at certain places, and these are always closed at night; and, in the case of any disturbance, during the day, should occasion require it.

Behind the town, on the hillside, there are many large Buddhist temples and gardens. These are placed in the best situations. The view over the town, the bay, and the distant hills is most charming, and well repays the visitor for the toil of the ascent. Camphor trees of a great size were common about these temples. They were apparently of great age, and were the finest examples of this tree I had were. The *Pinus Chinense*, or *P. Massoniana* was also common, and attains a great size. Higher up, the hillsides were covered with many thousands of tombstones, marking the tombs of generations who have long since passed away. This large cemetery forms a prominent object in the landscape, and presents a striking and curious appearance to the stranger who looks upon it for the first time.

One day, during my walks in Nagasaki, I had an opportunity of seeing some extraordinary processions. The first one I saw consisted of a number of men dressed up as Chinamen, who were supporting a huge dragon, and making it wriggle about in an extraordinary manner. Another procession consisted of little children, some so small that they could hardly walk, who were dressed in the Dutch military costume—cocked hats, tailed coats with epaulets, dress swords, and everything in the first style, closely resembling *mynheer* on gala-days, when the trade of Japan was all his own, and Deshima—dear little prison—his abiding place. In this procession, Dutch fraus and frauleins were duly represented, and truth compels me to say that they were never shown off to more advantage. The procession was accompanied by a band, dressed up also in an appropriate manner: they had European instruments, and played European music. The day was fine; thousands of people lined the streets, flags were hung from every window, and altogether the scene was most amusing.

I followed the procession through the principal streets, and then up to a large temple situated on the hillside above the town. Here the infantine troop was put through various military maneuvers, which were executed in a most creditable manner. I was amused at the gravity with which everything was done—each child looked as if it was ill sober earnest, and scarcely a smile played on one of the many little faces that were taking part in this mimic representation of the good Dutchmen. The exercises having been gone through, the band struck up a lively air, and the little actors marched away to their homes.

On the side of a hill, a few miles out of Nagasaki, and amongst the most beautiful scenery, lives the veteran naturalist, Philipp Franz Von Siebold. His house is some distance away from that of any other European; and his delight seems to be in his garden, his library, and the Japanese country people who are his friends. As I had decided to pay him a visit during my stay in Nagasaki, I chose a fine day, and set out in the direction of his residence after breakfast.

My road led me through the heart of the town. The streets, as I have already remarked, were wide and clean, and contrasted most favorably with towns of equal size in China. The common necessaries of life seemed to be abundant everywhere. Amongst fruits I observed the *Diospyros kaki* pears, oranges, *Salisburia* nuts, chestnuts, water melons, acorns, &c. The vegetables consisted of carrots, onions, nelumbium roots, turnips, lily roots, ginger, *Arum esculentum*, yams, sweet potatoes, and a root called *gobbo*, apparently a species of Arctium.

After passing through the town the road led mo up a beautiful rice valley, terraced in all directions and watered abundantly by the streams that flow from the mountains. On each side of the valley the hills are richly wooded, partially with trees and partially with brushwood. The trees I observed were *Pinus Massoniana Cryptomeria, Retinosporay camphor*, oaks, camellias, &c. The view from one side, looking down upon and over the valley, and resting on the opposite hill, is rich indeed, and I almost envied Von Siebold his residence, which is situated on the left-hand side going up the valley. I found him at home, and he received me most kindly. His house is a good one for Japan, and his workshop or library, to which he introduced me, contains works of all countries on his favorite pursuits connected with natural history. But it was to the garden that my attention was more particularly drawn.

On a level with the house and around it are small nurseries for the reception and propagation of new plants, and for preparing them for transportation to Europe. Here I noted examples of most of the plants figured and described in Von Siebold's great work, the *Flora Japonica*, so well known to all lovers of oriental plants; and several new things hitherto undescribed. A new Aucuba with white blotches on the leaves was striking; there was also the male variety of the old *A. japonica* numerous fine conifers, such as *Thujopsis dolabrata, Sciadopitys verticillata, Betinospora pisifera* and *R. ohtusa*, and many other objects of interest. Plants with variegated foliage were numerous, and many of them were very beautiful. Amongst the latter I may mention *Thujas, Eleagnus*, Junipers, bamboos, *Podocarpus*, Camellias, *Euryas*, &c.

On the hillside above the house, Von Siebold is clearing away the brushwood in order to extend his collections and to obtain suitable situations for the different species to thrive in. For example, he will have elevation for such plants as require it, shade and dampness for others, and so on. Long may he live to delight himself and others with his enlightened pursuits!

Von Siebold speaks the Japanese language like a native, and appears to be a great favorite with the people around him, amongst whom he has great influence. "Doctor," said I to him on taking my leave, "you appear to be quite a prince amongst the people in this part of Japan." He smiled and said he liked the Japanese, and he believed the regard was mutual; and with a slight cast of sarcasm in his countenance, continued, "It is not necessary for me to

carry a revolver in my belt, like the good people in Deshima and Nagasaki."
During my stay in Nagasaki at this time I was greatly indebted to Joseph
Evans, of the well-known house of Dent and Co., of China. Edward Webb,
the head of that house in Shanghai, kindly furnished me with letters of introduction and credit; so that even "at the ends of the earth" I found myself
quite at home. Evans introduced me to a number of native gentlemen whose
gardens were rich in the botanical productions of Japan; and I am glad to
take this opportunity of stating, that to him and to Mackenzie I am indebted
for many important additions to my collections. Everywhere we were
received with the most marked politeness by the Japanese—a politeness I
am vain enough to think we did not abuse in the slightest degree.

I have already stated that according to treaty foreigners are now allowed
to visit the country in the vicinity of the ports that have been opened to
trade. The distance allowed is ten *ri*, or some twenty-five to thirty miles.
I was not slow to avail myself of this liberty in order to examine the natural
products and agriculture of the country. Day by day excursions were made,
either on foot or on horseback. One of these was to a place called Ebisu,
a kind of picnic station amongst the hills, about four or five miles from the
town. The summer agricultural productions of the country through which
I passed were much like those in the province of Zhejiang in China—that
is, rice and *Artim escvlentum* on the low lands, and sweet potatoes, buckwheat
(*Polygonum iataricum*), maize, &c., on the dry hilly soil. In winter, wheat,
barley, and rape are produced on the dry lands, and the rice-lands are
generally allowed to lie fallow.

On the hillsides I observed the Japan waxtree (*Rhus succedaneum*)
cultivated extensively. It occupies the same position on these hills as the
Chinese tallow tree (*Stillhigia sehiferd*) floes in Zhejiang. It grows to about
the same size and, curiously enough, it produces the same effect on the
autumnal landscape by its leaves changing from green into a deep bloodred color as they ripen before falling off. I saw some camphor trees (*Lauras
camphora*) of enormous size about the temples on the outskirts of Nagasaki,
and *Cryptomeria japonica* was a very common tree on all the hillsides. The
latter is often used as a fence round gardens, and a very pretty one it makes.
When I first saw it used for this purpose, it struck me that something of
the same kind might be done with it at home, now that it is so common

in every nursery. The Japanese manage it much in the same way as we do our yew hedges; and when kept regularly clipped it is not only exceedingly pretty, but it also is so dense that nothing can get through it. The tea-plant is also common on these hillsides, but the great tea region of Japan is 200 or 300 miles further to the northward, near famous Kyoto, where the emperor resides.

At this season the tea was just coming into flower, so that I was enabled to procure specimens for the herbarium. It is no doubt identical with the China plant, and may have been introduced from China; although, as the productions of the two countries are very similar in character, it may be indigenous. In its mode of growth and habits it resembles the plant in cultivation about Canton, commonly called *Thea bohea*.

Ebisu, to which I was bound while making these observations, was reached in due course. I found the proprietor had a nice little private garden, and also a nursery in which he propagated and cultivated plants for sale. On the premises there was a building, apparently for the use of foreigners, which was only opened when any foreigner came out from Nagasaki for a day's pleasure. Like many other places of the kind, its walls were defaced with the writing of the great men who had visited it, and who took this means of immortalizing themselves. Doggrel lines, some of them scarcely fit to meet the eye, were observed in many places written in Dutch, German, or Russian. Our own countrymen had not been there long enough to visit the place and leave their marks; doubtless these will be found also in good time.

The nursery garden at Ebisu was found to contain a large collection of Japanese plants—some of which were new to me—and others of great rarity and interest. Several species were purchased for my collection, and duly brought in to the town the next day.

Having finished my examination of the nursery, I started, in company with some other gentlemen, on an expedition to the top of Inasa-*yama*, a hill some 1500 feet above the level of the sea, and celebrated for the fine and extensive view to be obtained from its summit. It was a glorious autumnal day, such a day as one rarely sees in our own changeable climate. The sky was cloudless, so that when we reached the top our view on all sides was bounded only by the horizon. Looking to the south-east, far below us we saw the town of Nagasaki, with the beautiful bay in its front. On its smooth waters were the ships of several nations at anchor, besides a number of boats and junks of native build, and rather picturesque in their way. Turning round and looking to the north-west, the eye rested on many hundreds of little hills having a conical form, and covered to their summits with trees and brushwood. Behind them were mountains, apparently 2000 or 3000 feet in height, and a deep bay looking like an inland sea. Amongst the hills there were many beautiful and fertile valleys, now yellow with the ripening rice crops; and numerous villages and farmhouses gave life to the scene, which was one of extraordinary beauty and interest.

On our way home we visited a little garden belonging to an interpreter to the Japanese government. Here again I noticed some azaleas remarkable for their great size, and an extraordinary specimen of a dwarfed fir tree. Its lower branches were trained horizontally some twenty feet in length; all the leaves and branchlets were tied down and clipped, so that the whole was as flat as a board. The upper branches were trained to form circles one above another like so many little tables, and the whole plant had a most curious appearance. A man was at work on it at the time, and I believe it keeps him constantly employed every day throughout the year!

Since the opening of the port of Nagasaki to other nations besides the Chinese and Dutch, its trade has been greatly enlarged. The harbour is now gay with the ships of all nations, and a brisk trade has sprung up between Japan and China—a trade which the quiet old Dutchmen never seemed to have dreamed of. Large quantities of seaweed, salt fish, and sundry other articles are exported to China; while the Chinese import medicine of various kinds, Sapan wood, and many other kinds of dyes. The exports to Europe are chiefly tea, vegetable wax (the produce of the Rhus already noticed), and copper, which is found in large quantities in the Japanese islands. At present there is little demand for our English manufactures, but that may spring up in time. Although Nagasaki may never become a place of very great importance as regards trade, it will no doubt prove one of the most healthy stations in the East; and may one day become most valuable as a sanatarium for our troops in that quarter of the globe.

To Yokohama

Leaving Nagasaki and its beautiful scenery at daylight on the 19th of October, we proceeded on our voyage to the port of Yokohama, near Edo, the capital of Japan, and distant from Nagasaki about 700 miles. When outside the harbour of Nagasaki the mariner has two courses open to him: he may either go northward, and pass through the Straits of Shimonoseki and through the Inland Sea that divides the islands of Honshu and Shikoku, or he may take a southerly course and go through Van Diemen's Strait [Ōsumi Kaikyō], and thus out into the waters of the Pacific Ocean. Sailing vessels generally choose the latter, as being the safer and more expeditious way of reaching their destination, and this was the *Marmora*'s course in the present instance. Luckily we had a fair wind all the way from Nagasaki until we got through the strait. Near the entrance to the strait there are some small islands known to mariners as the Retribution Rocks [Tsukura-se]. They are only a few feet above the water, and are rather dangerous neighbors in a dark night, or during those heavy gales for which this coast is so unfavorably known. On our left we observed the mainland of Kyushu, stretching far away to the eastward, and ending in a cape named Cape Chichakoff [Sata no Misaki]. A high conical-shaped mountain named Horner Peak [Kaimondake], 2345 feet in height, and not unlike Fuji-*yama* in miniature, was also passed on our left. It forms an excellent landmark to the navigator of these seas. Between Horner Peak and the cape there is a deep bay jutting inland for 30 or 40 miles, and having at its head an important city named Kagoshima, where the *daimyō* of Satsuma has his head-quarters. On the south side of the strait we observed several large islands, one of which is named Iōjima, or Sulphur Island. This is an active volcano, and smoke and flames are continually rising, not from its summit in the usual way, but from many parts of its sides. The whole mountain seems on fire, and has a very curious appearance when seen during the night.

The coast of Japan is remarkable for the suddenness with which gales of wind come on, and we were now destined to have our turn. It was a beautiful eveningwhen we were nearly abreast of Cape Chichakoff; we had a light fair wind, and our little bark was gliding along at the rate of six or seven miles an hour. We were congratulating ourselves on our great good luck, and just coming to the conclusion that all we had heard and read of the gales on this coast were so many travellers' stories; but we were soon compelled to come to a different conclusion. Towards dark the sky began to wear a lowering appearance in the north-east, and in less than half an hour we were in the midst of a gale of wind. Sail after sail was taken in, and at last it was deemed advisable to lie to until some change in the weather should take place. The sea also rose with great rapidity, and, except in a typhoon in China, I never recollect such a gale and such a sea. Our little bark behaved admirably, rising and falling with the sea, and shipping comparatively little water.

For two days it was necessary for us to remain in this uncomfortable position; and when the gale moderated, and we were able to get a little sail upon the vessel, the winds were foul, and carried us considerably to the southward of our course. But it cannot always blow a gale, even in Japan; so, whether the winds were tired of persecuting us, or whether it was owing to the influence of sundry old shoes which were thrown overboard, I cannot say, but the gale ceased, and a fair wind sprang up from the westward. On the evening of the 28th we were abreast of Cape Irozaki, at the head of the Izu Peninsula—that cape of storms where it is said to blow always. Our experience, however, was rather different; for we seemed to run into a dead calm, with a heavy tumbling sea.

At daybreak on the 29th we were opposite a group of islands situated not very far from the entrance to the Bay of Edo. One of them—Vries's Island [Ōshima]—rises to the height of 2530 feet above the sea, and has an active volcano on its summit. The smoke, which continuously rises from this mountain, forms an excellent landmark for mariners approaching this part of the coast. As we sailed past we observed that on the sides of the mountain, and particularly down near the shore, there were numerous villages and small towns. There were apparently some fertile valleys and hillsides at a low elevation, but near the summit all appeared barren, while huge volumes of smoke were seen following each other at short intervals.

On our left, on that same morning, was spread out to our admiring gaze the fair land of Japan; and very beautiful it was to look upon. The land was hilly and mountainous as in China; but there appeared, some fifty or sixty miles inland. Mount Fuji, or Fuji-*yama*, the Matchless, or Holy Mountain of the Japanese. Its northern slopes were covered with snow, but on its southern sides green streaks of verdure were visible. This mountain is the highest in Japan. It was formerly supposed to be only 10,000 or 12,000 feet above the level of the sea, but later observations made by Alcock's party in 1860 give it a height of 14,177 feet.

In the evening we passed Cape Sagami at the entrance of the Bay of Edo, and at daybreak next morning we were well up the bay, and only a short distance from the Yokohama anchorage. On our right, in the direction of Edo, we observed a cloud of boats under sail, composed chiefly of which supply the markets of the capital and the surrounding towns with fish. During our voyage from Nagasaki, I had observed very few native vessels or fishing boats, such as may be seen crowding the waters of the Chinese coast. In so far as seagoing vessels are concerned, I was quite prepared to see but few, as the Japanese are not a maritime nation, and do not send ships to foreign countries; but I fully expected to see fleets of fishing boats along the shore, and their absence leads me to doubt whether the Japanese islands are as populous as they are generally supposed to be.

We anchored abreast of the town of Yokohama at eight o'clock on the morning of the 30th of October. This is one of the ports opened by treaty to foreigners, and it is the one nearest to the capital. It was here that in March, 1854, Commodore Perry, of the United States Navy, concluded his treaty with the Japanese. At one of the interviews presents were delivered from the American government. These consisted of American cloths, agricultural implements, firearms, and a beautiful locomotive, tender, and passenger car, one-fourth of the ordinary size. The latter was put in motion on a circular track, and went at the rate of twenty miles an hour. The Japanese, we are told, were more interested in this than in anything else; but, Chinese-like, concealed all expressions of wonder or astonishment.

The town of Kanagawa, farther north along the bay, is the place named as the port in the treaty, but it was found unsuitable owing to the shallowness of the water all along that part of the shore. For a long time the ministers and consuls of the treaty powers endeavored to induce their respective merchants to abstain from renting land or building on the Yokohama side of the bay. Curiously enough the Japanese government took a different view of the matter, and encouraged the merchants to come to Yokohama by building for them dwelling houses, and commodious piers and landing places.

Both places had their advantages and disadvantages. The argument of the consuls in favor of adhering to Kanagawa was that it was on the great highway of Japan; and that, as Japanese from all parts of the empire were daily passing through it, our merchandise would, through them, be carried to all parts of the country, and would in this manner be quickly known and appreciated. It was also hinted that the government intended to hem foreigners in at Yokohama by means of a broad and deep canal; that this in fact was to be another Deshima; and that we were to be made prisoners and treated in all respects as the Dutch were in the olden time at Nagasaki.

The advantage of Kanagawa being on the Tōkaidō, the great highway of Japan, was fully admitted by the merchants, but they believed that if they located themselves there the government would lead the main road round by some other way, and would take measures to have them and their Japanese customers as much under control as at Yokohama. As to the latter place being made a second Deshima, they argued that the time had gone by when such things were possible. Besides, if Kanagawa was chosen, the ships would have to lie a long way from the shore, where they would oftentimes be unapproachable owing to the state of the weather, which is very uncertain on this coast. Altogether Yokohama was the most suitable place for the transaction of their business, and it was business that had brought them to Japan.

While this discussion was going on, the Japanese government, for reasons of its own, was affording every facility to those who wished to settle at

Yokohama; and notwithstanding the opposition of the ministers and consuls of the treaty powers, the merchants carried their point. Unhappily all this was the cause of much wrangling and ill feeling, which it will take some time to remove.

When the American squadron first visited Yokohama in 1854, it was but a small fishing village, containing probably not more than 1000 inhabitants. Now the population amounts to 18,000 or 20,000, and a large town covers a space formerly occupied by ricefields and vegetable gardens. The town is built on the flat land that extends along the shores of the bay, and is backed by a kind of semicircle of low richly-wooded hills. It is about a mile long, and a quarter to half a mile in width; but it is increasing rapidly every day, and no doubt the whole of the swamp that lies between it and the hills will soon be covered with buildings.

A large customhouse has been erected near the centre of the town, the foreign allotments being on the east side of it, and the native town chiefly on the west, so that foreigners and natives are kept each by themselves. A broad and deep canal has been dug round the town, and is connected with the bay at each end. It will be seen, therefore, that with the sea in front, and this canal carried round behind, the place can easily be completely isolated. Guardhouses are placed at the points of egress, and no one can go out or come in without the knowledge of the guards, and consequently of the government. As I have already hinted, the Japanese have been much abused for this arrangement; but it is possible, indeed I think it highly probable, that it has been intended more for our protection than for anything else.

The new houses of the foreign merchants are generally one-storied bungalows, built almost entirely of wood and plaster. The joints of the timbers are tied together, or fastened in a way to allow the entire structure to rock or move to and fro during those earthquakes that are so common and sometimes so destructive in this part of the world. Godowns for the storing of merchandise are generally erected near the house of the merchant; and in many instances there is also a fireproof building on the premises, used for the protection of specie and the more valuable portion of the merchant's property. This is of the first importance in a country like Japan, where the buildings are so combustible in their nature, and where fires are almost a daily occurrence in all the large towns. The native town is remarkable for one fine wide street running down its centre. Here are exposed for sale the various products of the country in very large quantities. Bronzes, carvings in ivory, lacquerware, and porcelain, are all duly represented. The bronzes are mostly modem, of ugly shapes, and are chiefly remarkable for the large quantity of metal they contain, which one would think might have been applied to a more useful purpose. The small ivory carvings and metal buckles for fastening the dress are great curiosities in their way. They are usually small, and represent men, women, monkeys, and all sorts of animals and plants. They exhibit the skill of the carver in a very favorable light, and are certainly wonderful examples of patience and industry. Some collections of these articles were shown in the late International Exhibition in London, and were much admired. A writer in *The Times* describes them in the following terms:

> The designs in some of these metal buckles are irresistibly grotesque, and at once recall to mind the little black woodcuts with which Leech began his connexion with *Punch*. Probably every object in this collection is by a different artist; yet, though in some the designs are so minute as to require a magnifying glass to see them well, all are treated with the same broad humor, so that it is almost impossible to avoid downright laughter as you examine them. There is one figure of a man timidly venturing to coax a snarling dog, which is inimitable in its funny expression; and so also is the expression on another's face who is frightened by a ghost. And all these works, the reader must remember, are not mere sketches, but are solid little pieces of metal-work, the background being of bronze, and the raised figures in relief being either gold, silver, steel, or platinum, or, as in most cases, of all four metals intermixed. It is evident, from the platinum being so freely used here, that the metal must be much more common with the Japanese than with us; and that the secret of melting it, to which our chemical knowledge has only just attained, has long been known to them. … In the side of the case where the metal buckles are shown we find in a collection of ivory carvings fresh proofs of the art, skill, and comic genius of the people. Let anyone examine

the litter of puppies sprawling over each other, the grotesque look of pain on the face of the woman who has been startled by a fox, and tumbled forward with her fingers under the edge of a basin; the triumphant aspect of the companion figure, who has succeeded in clapping his basin down on the fox; yet, notwithstanding their wonderful finish, all these figures are so small that they might be worn as brooches.

The modern lacquerware is good, but not to be compared to the fine old Kyoto ware, which is extremely beautiful. There are a number of shops where this can be procured; but the prices asked, and obtained, are very high. The fine polish of the old lac is unrivalled, and the specimens are oftentimes covered with figures of gold. This ware is met with in the form of writing-boxes and boxes for holding papers, trays, cabinets, screens, &c. The finest pieces are often very small, and, although not of much use, are sufficient to show the high state of the art at the time when they were made.

I saw few examples of ancient porcelain, although we know that some fine pieces have found their way to Europe from Japan. The porcelain shops are full of modern ware, chiefly remarkable for the fine eggshell cups; and I found one or two examples of good coloring. Generally I did not admire it, and considered it not equal to that now made in China, and far inferior to the ancient porcelain of that country. I observed some cups and basins, with paintings of English ladies not badly executed. This shows how quick and imitative the Japanese are as a people, and how different they are from the slow-going Chinese.

In some of the shops I observed some large crystal-looking balls said to be of rock crystal. These were finely polished and clear—not a flaw of any kind could be detected in their structure—and were highly prized owing to their great size and beauty.

All sorts of toys were abundant, and some of them were most ingenious and pretty. There were glass balls, with numerous little tortoises inside them, whose heads, tails, and feet were in constant motion; humming-tops, with a number of trays inside, which all came out and spun round on the table when the top was set in motion; and a number of funny things in boxes like little bits of wood shavings, which perform the most curious antics when thrown into a basin containing water. Dolls of the most fascinating kind, with large, shaved, bobbing heads, crying out most lustily when pressed upon the stomach, were also met with in cartloads. One little article, so small one could scarcely see it, when put upon hot charcoal, gradually seemed to acquire life and animation, and moved about for all the world like a brilliant caterpillar. This large trade in toys shows us how fond the Japanese are of their children.

In one of the main streets there is a shop with an extensive collection of books, maps, charts, plain and colored, for sale. A good map of the city of Edo may be had here; but the inquirer for such a thing is invariably taken into a back room, when he is told that if the authorities knew of such a thing being sold the vendor would get his head taken off.[1] To those who are ignorant of the language, a peculiar motion of the hand about the region of the neck explains the shopkeeper's meaning. This is a good stroke of policy, as it enables the seller to obtain a higher price for the map, and sends the lucky purchaser off highly delighted with his bargain. In the same shop I met with some really good illustrated books, containing views of the country and people about Kyoto and Edo, the two most famous cities in Japan. The former is the residence of the *mikado* or emperor, and the latter that of the *shōgun*. In the art of drawing or sketching, the Japanese are far inferior to ourselves, but they are greatly in advance of the Chinese. Although foreigners have been only a short time residing in Yokohama, their appearance, customs, and manners are faithfully represented by the Japanese artists. Here are to be found pictures of men and women—rather caricatures it must be confessed—engaged in amusements peculiar to highly civilized nations. Ladies riding on horseback, or walking—duly encompassed with a wonderful amount of crinoline—are fairly represented. Scenes in the Gankirō—a place got up by the government for the amusement of foreigners—are also portrayed in a manner not particularly flattering to our habits and customs. Boisterous mirth, indulgence in wine and strong drinks, and the effects thereof upon those who are inclined to

---

1 It was exactly such a transaction that got Phillip Franz von Siebold into trouble during his first stay in Japan when, on 22 October 1829, the *bakufu* ordered him to leave Japan after it had learned he was in the possession of detailed maps of Japan and Korea from the hands of the famous Japanese cartographer Inō Tadataka.

be quarrelsome, are all carefully depicted. Altogether, some very curious and instructive works of Japanese art may be picked up in shops of this description.

Opposite to the bookshop just noticed there is a menagerie containing a variety of animals for sale. In this place I saw some extraordinary-looking monkeys, which appear to be a source of great attraction and amusement to the natives.

Little dogs were plentiful, and particularly noisy when a foreigner approached them. Then there were examples of deer, the eagle of the country, and singing birds of various kinds in cages. But the different varieties of fowls struck me more than anything else. The kind I had already seen at Nagasaki was here also, and in addition pure white bird with a fine long arched tail and long silky feathers hanging down from each side of the back. This is a very beautiful bird, and well worth being introduced into Europe if it is not already here.

The Gankirō, to which I have already alluded, is a large building at the back of the town, erected by the government for the amusement of foreigners. Here, dinners, suppers, and plays can always be got up on the shortest notice. In other respects this and the buildings in the surrounding neighbourhood are much like the teahouses in the town of Nagasaki. Scenes of debauchery and drunkenness are common, and even murder is not infrequent. Over such matters one would willingly draw a veil, but truth must be told in order to correct the impression some persons have of Japan—namely, that it is a very Garden of Eden, and its inhabitants as virtuous as Adam and Eve before the fall.

The countryside in the vicinity of Yokohama is very beautiful in its general features. It is evidently of volcanic origin. It consists of low hills and small valleys: the former having their sloping sides covered with trees and brushwood, and their summits, which form a kind of table-land, all under cultivation. The valleys are very fertile, and, having a good supply of water, are generally used for the cultivation of rice.

The geological structure of this part of Japan is well worthy of notice. In my walks in the country I came upon a little hill with perpendicular sides, thus forming a convenient object for observation. The following is its formation in layers:

1st layer: Vegetable soil: black, resembling peat
2nd layer: Sholls 2 to 3 feet in thickness. Oysters and other sea shells.
3rd layer: Gravel.
4th layer: Light-colonred clay, with pumice-stone and shells.
5th layer: Blueish-colonred clay, with pumice-stone and shells.

The Yokohama cliffs are from 60 to 100 feet in height, nearly perpendicular, and their structure is as follows:

1st layer: Black, peaty-looking soil.
2nd layer: Bed earth much mixed with gravel.
3rd layer: Gravel.
4th layer: Hard clay.

This is intersected here and there with a layer of gravel, and sometimes with a layer of shells, principally oysters. The shells are seen sticking on the surface of this layer in all directions. There was also charred wood and pumice-stone among the clay.

Springs of excellent water are abundant on all the hillsides. Some of them are deliciously cool even in the hottest days of summer, and afford a refreshing drought to the weary traveller.

Kanagawa

The post town of Kanagawa, named in the treaty as the location of foreigners, is situated on the northern side of a deep bay or inlet; Yokohama being placed on its southern shore. The consuls of the different treaty powers were living in temples on the Kanagawa side at the time of my arrival; and as an old friend of mine, Joséh Loureira, the manager for Dent and Co., of China, who was also consul for Portugal and France, was residing there, he kindly offered me quarters in his temple during my stay. Nothing could have suited me better than this arrangement. There was plenty of room, both in the house and in the garden, for any collections of natural history I might get together; and I was on the Tōkaidō, the old highway to Edo, and in the midst of a most fertile and interesting country.

Kanagawa is a long narrow town stretching for several miles along the shore of the bay, and having one principal street, and that is the Tōkaidō, or the great eastern highway of Japan. The place is mentioned in the books of the old Dutch travellers, and is said by them to contain about six hundred houses, and to be twenty-four miles from the capital. It is probably about this distance from Nihonbashi in Edo, from which distances are measured to all parts of the empire; but it is not more than sixteen or eighteen miles from the western end of the city of Edo. It contains a great number of inns and teahouses; and here the Dutch generally slept on the last night of their journey overland from Nagasaki to Edo. On the following day they entered the capital. The shops are generally poor and mean, and contain few articles except the mere necessaries of life. A little way back from the main street, at intervals all the way along the town, are Buddhist temples and cemeteries.

These temples are often found in the most charming situations, and they are the finest and most substantial buildings in Kanagawa. In some instances they are surrounded with pretty gardens, containing specimens of the favorite flowers of the country. It is in some of these temples that the consuls of the treaty powers have been located. The good priests do not object to find quarters of an inferior kind both for themselves and for their gods, providing they are well paid for their trouble in turning out.

The Tōkaidō is thronged all day long with people going to or returning from the capital. Every now and then a long train of the servants and armed retainers of one of the *daimyō*—lords or *daimyō* of the empire—may be seen covering the road for miles. It is not unusual for a cortege of this kind to occupy two or three hours in passing by. Men run before and call upon the people to fall down upon their knees to do honor to the great man, nor do they call in vain. All the people on both sides of the way drop down instantly on their knees, and remain in this posture until the *norimono* or palanquin of the *daimyō* has passed by. A *daimyō*'s procession is made up in the following manner: first comes the *daimyō* himself in his *norimono*,[1] followed by his horse and retainers, armed with swords, spears, and matchlocks; then follow a number of coolies, each carrying two lacquered boxes slung across his shoulder on a bamboo pole. After these again there is another *norimono*, with an official of some kind; then more coolies with boxes, more retainers, and so on. The number of the followers is often very large, and depends upon and is regulated by the wealth and rank of the *daimyō*.

Kaempfer informs us:

> that it is the duty of the *daimyō* of the empire, as also of the governors of imperial cities and crown lands, to go to court once a year to pay their homage and respect. They are attended, going and returning, by their whole court, and travel with a pomp and magnificence, becoming as well their own quality and riches as the majesty of the powerful monarch whom they are going to see. The train of some of the most eminent fills up the road for some days.

---

1 In fact, the *daimyō*'s palanquin was the second one, at the center of the procession. The first, more sober, palanquin was usually that of the so-called *sendōyaku*, the retainer in charge of 'leading the way.'

If two or more of these *daimyō* should chance to be travelling along the same road, at the same time, they would prove a great hindrance to one another, particularly if they should happen to meet at the same post-house or village. This is avoided by giving timely notice, and by engaging the inns and post-houses a month or six weeks beforehand. The time of their intended arrival is also notified in all the cities, villages, and hamlets, by putting up small boards on high poles of bamboo, signifying in a few characters what day of the month such and such a lord will be at that place to dine and sleep there.

When the retinue of the great man has passed by, the stream of every-day life flows on along the great Tōkaidō as before. No carts are used on this part of the road. Everything is carried on packhorses, and these are passing along the road in great numbers all day long. Each horse is loaded with a pile of boxes and packages—a formidable size oftentimes, surmounted by a man in a large broad-brimmed straw hat, who, from his exalted position, is guiding the movements of his horse. Generally, however, when passing through towns, the horses are led by the drivers. In addition to the huge pile of packages, it is not unusual for a little family, consisting of the mother and children, to be housed amongst them. On one occasion, as two foreigners of my acquaintance were out riding in the country, one of their horses shied, and, coming in contact with a loaded pack-horse, its burden came tumbling off, and was scattered over the road. On stopping to render the driver some assistance in reloading his horse, my friends were horrified to find a whole family scrabbling about amongst the packages, amongst which they had been snugly stowed away.

Besides the processions, packhorses, and palanquins, the pedestrians on the Tōkaidō demand our attention. Some are crowned with queer-looking broad-brimmed straw hats; others have napkins tied round their heads, and their hats slung behind their backs, only to be used when it rains or when the sun's rays are disagreeably powerful; while others again have the head bare and shaven in front, with the little pigtail (*chonmage*) brought forward and tied down upon the crown. Mendicant priests are met with, chanting prayers at every door, jingling some rings on the top of a tall staff, and begging for alms for the support of themselves and their temples. These are most independent-looking fellows, and seem to think themselves conferring a favor rather than receiving one. I observed that they were rarely refused alms by the people, although the same priests came round almost daily. To me the prayer seemed to be always the same—namely, *nam-nam-nam*;[2] sometimes sung in a low key, and sometimes in a high one. When the little copper cash—the coin of the country—was thrown into the tray of the priest, he gave one more prayer, apparently for the charity he had received, jingled his rings, and then went on to the next door. Blind men are also common, who give notice of their approach by making a peculiar sound upon a reed. These men generally get their living by shampooing their more fortunate brethren who can see. Every now and then a group of sturdy beggars, each having an old straw mat thrown across his shoulders, come into the stream which flows along this great highway.

Then there is the flower-dealer, with his basket of pretty flowers, endeavoring to entice the ladies to purchase them for the decoration of their hair; or with his branches of *Shikimi* (*Illicium aniatum*) and other evergreens, which are largely used to ornament the tombs of the dead.

All day long, and during a great part of the night too, this continual living stream flows to and from the great capital of Japan along the imperial highway. It forms a panorama of no common kind, and is certainly one of the great sights of the empire. The blind travellers, of whom there are a great number, are said to prefer travelling by night when the road is less crowded, as the light of day makes no difference to them.

Having settled down for a time in Kanagawa, I now made daily excursions to different parts of the surrounding country. I was fortunate in making the acquaintance of the Samuel Robbins Brown, a missionary connected with the Dutch Reformed Church, United States, and of Charles Hepburn, a medical missionary, formerly of Amoy, in China. They were living in some temples a short distance from where I was lodging; and as they had been some time in Japan, they were able to give me much valuable information.

My first question was, whether there were any large Buddhist temples in this part of Japan, similar to those I had been in the habit of visiting in China. My reason for wishing to get information on this head was that,

2 Pura land monks chanted *Namu Amida Butsu* (Homage to the Buddha), while Nmichiren monks chanted *Namu Myōhō Renge-kyō* (Homage to the True Dharma of the Lotus Sūtra).

wherever Buddhist temples and Buddhist priests are found, there the timber is preserved on the hillsides; and many of the rare trees of the country are sure to be met with adorning some of the courts of their temples. Brown informed me that there was a large monastery a short distance up one of the valleys, and kindly consented to accompany me. Our road led us up a beautiful and fertile valley, having low wooded hills on each side, and a little stream of pure water running down towards the sea, watering arid fertilizing the ricefields on its way. It was now the beginning of November, and the crops were yellow and nearly ready for the reaping-hook of the farmer. It was a glorious autumnal day, the sun was shining above our heads in a clear sky, the air was cool, and everything around us was most enjoyable.

A walk of two or three miles brought us to the Bugen temple. A broad path led up the hillside to the main entrance of the temple. Various ornamental trees, some of great size and beauty, stood near the gateway. Just inside and in front of one of the principal temples, I was delighted to meet with a beautiful new pine, called *Sciadopitys verticillata* the umbrella pine, or *Koya-maki*—that is, "the *maki* of Mount Koya"—of the Japanese. A branch of this fine tree is figured and described in Von Siebold's *Flora Japonica*; but a great mistake is made as regards its size. Siebold states that it forms an evergreen tree, for the most part twelve to fifteen feet high. On the contrary, the specimens met with in the vicinity of Kanagawa and Edo were in many instances fully one hundred feet in height. However, as Siebold says that he saw it cultivated in gardens, he probably had no opportunity of seeing a full-grown specimen. It is a tree of great beauty and interest. It has broad leaves of a deep green color, arranged in whorls, each somewhat like a parasol, and is quite unlike any other genus amongst conifers. In general outline it is of a conical form, not spreading, and the branches and leaves are so dense that the stem is completely hidden from view. It is impossible to say, until we have further experience, whether this fine tree will prove hardy in our English climate; but if it does so, it will be a very great acquisition to our list of ornamental pines.

The principal hall of the Bugen-*ji* is not remarkable either for its size or for its idols. But the hillside is covered with small detached buildings, which appear to be not only residences but also seminaries for the Buddhist priesthood. These houses are situated in the midst of pretty gardens, each of which contains neat specimens, well cultivated, of the ornamental flowers of the country, and is surrounded with hedges kept neatly clipped and trimmed. The whole place is kept in the highest order, the broad walks are daily swept, and not a weed or dead leaf is to be seen anywhere.

At a higher elevation there are some large temples, which seem to be kept always closed. They are rather rough wooden buildings; but like all the other temples are beautifully thatched, and the ground and walks near them clean and in perfect order. We did not observe any priests near these temples; and they probably belong to the sect of Shintō, the original national religion of Japan, upon which Buddhism has been engrafted in some extraordinary manner.

It the time of our visit to the monastery, the priests seemed all to be engaged in study or in prayer. Now and then the dull monotonous sound of someone of them engaged with his devotions fell on our ears, but it soon ceased and all was still again. The sun was shining, and its rays streaming through the branches of the overhanging trees; a solemn stillness seemed to reign around us, and the whole place and scene reminded one of a sabbath in the country at home.

There are many pleasant and shaded walks in the woods about these temples. Taking one of the paths leading up the hill, we wandered to the summit and obtained some charming views. On one side we looked down on the roofs and gardens of the temples, and our eyes wandered from them over the valley to the richly wooded hills beyond. Turning to the westward, the mountains of Hakone lay before us, with the beautiful Fuji-*yama* half-covered with snow, and looking like the queen of the mountain scenery. These were glorious views, and will long remain vividly impressed on my memory.

Before quitting the monastery of Bugen-*ji*, we examined minutely the manner in which the temples were built, and more particularly their thatched roofs. The walls were formed of a framework of wood nicely fitted and joined, but apparently not very massive in construction. This was rather extraordinary, owing to the great thickness and weight of the framework of the roof. No doubt the sides were strong enough to support the roof, heavy though it was. All the roofs of the temples were thatched with a reed common to the country, and never, in any other part of the world, have I seen such beautiful thatching. Indeed this is a subject of admiration with every foreigner who visits Japan. On carefully examining the structure of one of these buildings, one soon sees the principles on which it is put up, and the reasons for its peculiar construction. Buildings such as we erect in England would be very unsafe in a country like Japan, where earthquakes are so common and so violent. Hence the main part of a Japanese house is a sort of skeleton framework; every beam is tied or fastened to its neighbor; so that, when the earth is convulsed by these fearful commotions, the whole building may rock and sway together without tumbling down. In order to render these buildings more secure, it seems necessary to have the roof of great strength and weight, and this accounts for their heavy and massive structure.

In the woods of this part of Japan there is a very fine elm, called by the Japanese *Keyaki* (*Zelkova serrata*). This is often used in the formation of the strong beams which support the roofs of these temples. The wood of this tree is extremely handsome; and as all the framework is fully exposed to view, this is, of course, a matter of great importance.

On our way home we visited many of the little farmhouses situated at short intervals on the lower sides of the hills. Each had its little garden attached to it. In one of these gardens we found a very fine collection of chrysanthemums. I was most anxious to secure some of them for my collections, but, thinking the farmer only cultivated them for his pleasure, I did not like to offer him money, nor did I care to beg. My scruples were soon set at rest by the owner hinting that I might have any I pleased by paying for them at a certain rate. I need scarcely say we soon came to terms, and in a very short space of time the little farmer, with his flowers on his back, was trudging behind us on our way to Kanagawa. This was my first purchase in Japan, and I lost no time in making the following note, namely, that the Japanese were very much like their Chinese friends over the water, and that no difficulty was so great that it could not be overcome by a little liberality.

My next object was to procure a native of this part of the country to assist me with my collections, and more particularly to act as a guide. A man named Tomi was recommended to me as a person likely to suit my purpose. Tomi had been a kind of pedler, and had wandered up and down the country for many years. Everybody knew Tomi, and Tomi knew everybody. Latterly he had been in the service of some foreigners at Kanagawa, who gave him a high character for intelligence and activity. But it was rumored that Tomi had, in common, 1 am sorry to say, with many of his countrymen, one serious fault, and that was, he was particularly fond of *sake*—the wine of Japan. It was added, however, that he rarely indulged until the evening, and that he was generally to be depended upon during the day. As his knowledge of the country was of great importance in my investigations, I thought he would perhaps suit me better than anyone else, and so I engaged him.

Tomi was now my daily guide all over the country, and I must do him the justice to say he performed his work to my entire satisfaction. In the mornings he looked rather red about the eyes, as if he had been indulging freely during the preceding night; but he kept sober, for the most part, during the day.

The weather was delightful; day after day the sun was shining in a clear sky, the air was cool, and I could walk all day long with the greatest comfort. The seeds of the different trees and shrubs of the country were now ripening; and my great object was to secure a supply of all the ornamental kinds for exportation to Europe. More particularly I wanted to procure seeds of the *Sciadopitys* already described, of the *Thujopsis dolabrata*, and of the different pines, yews, and arborvitae.

One morning Tomi informed me he had found out a temple in the country where there were some fine trees of *Thujopsis dolabrata*. This was good news; so we started off together to see the trees, and if possible to procure some seeds. Our road led us up a valley somewhat like that by which I had gone to the Bugen-*ji*. The scenery was of the same beautiful character—fertile valleys and richly wooded hills, which even at this time of the year (November) had a green and summerlike appearance, owing to the number of evergreen trees and shrubs indigenous to the country. Sometimes our road gradually ascended, leading us along the tops of the hills, which here form a kind of table-land, the whole of which is under cultivation. It is impossible for me to describe the beautiful views that were continually presenting themselves as we passed along. Looking seaward, the smooth waters of Edo Bay lay before us, dotted all over with the little white sails of fishing boats, whose produce supply the market of that populous capital. Strange ships, of another build and rig, lay quietly at anchor abreast of Yokohama. Their tall masts and square yards proclaimed them to belong to the nations of the West. Looking inland, the view from the hilltops was ever-changing but always interesting and beautiful. Rice valleys, farmhouses, and temples lay below us; beyond them were low hills, then valleys again, and so on, until the eye rested on a sea of hills on the far-off horizon.

A walk of a few miles brought us to a little temple nestled amongst some woods on a hillside. The name of this temple was Tōrin-*ji*. A small avenue of trees led up from a rice valley to the temple, and ended at a flight of stone steps. On each side of the steps there was a grassy bank covered with bushes of azalea, aucuba, and other ornamental shrubs. Ascending the stone steps we found ourselves on a level with the temple, and in a pretty garden filled with flowers, and kept in the most perfect order.

The temple of Tōrin-*ji* is a small one, and has only one priest and priestess to minister at its altars. It is cleanly kept, the floors are covered with mats, and many of the walls are ornamented with pictures. Works of art are highly appreciated by these people; and I afterwards, at their urgent request, presented them with some pictures from *Punch* and the *Illustrated London News*, with which they were highly pleased. The priest and priestess received us most kindly, and, as they appeared to be well acquainted with Tomi, we soon found ourselves quite at home. The screens of the little verandah were drawn, and we were invited to seat ourselves on the clean mats that covered the floor. Some delicious tea, made, in Chinese fashion, without milk or sugar, was set before us, and proved very agreeable.

While we sipped our tea I had time to make some observations on the surrounding scenery. A quiet and secluded rice valley formed the foreground to the picture; hills were on each side of us and behind us, densely covered with trees of many different kinds. Pines, evergreen oaks, chesnuts, bamboos, and palms—the latter giving a somewhat tropical character to the scenery—were the most common species. On a hillside to the right of where we sat I observed a grove of the beautiful *Thujopsis dolabrata* which I had come to look for.

A stillness, almost solemn, reigned amongst these woods and temples, broken at times only by the call of the cock pheasant, or the rich clear note of some songster of the woods. What a charming place for a hermit, or for someone tired of the busy scenes and oppressing cares of the world!

But I had not come here to meditate only; and setting down my teacup, I intimated to the good priest that I wished to pay a closer visit to the *Asunarō* the Japanese name for *Thujopsis dolabrata*. The old man kindly led the way. On arriving at the grove of these trees we found an old cemetery amongst them; and they had, no doubt, been planted there, along with a number of *Cryptotaenia* at the time the cemetery was first made.

The *Asunarō* is a beautiful tree, straight, symmetrical, attaining a height of 80 to 100 feet and having leaves of a fine dark-green color. They are imbricated, or overlap each other on the stems, and look almost as if they had been plaited. Beneath they are of a silvery hue, which gives them a somewhat remarkable appearance when blown about by the wind. We could observe some bunches of seeds on some of the higher branches. These were not very easily reached; but both Tomi and I being good climbers, we pulled off our shoes and mounted the trees, much to the astonishment of our good friend the priest, who stood quietly looking on at our proceedings.

The afternoon was far advanced before we had completed our researches in the vicinity of the Tōrin temple, and therefore, bidding adieu to the priest and priestess, we took our departure, choosing on our homeward journey a different road from that by which we came. As this road led us through a number of highly-cultivated valleys, I noted the state of the crops. The low rice-lands were now covered with that grain, yellow, and nearly ready for the sickle. On all the higher lands the young wheat and barley crops were now (Nov. 10th) above-ground. The seed is not sown broadcast as with us, but in rows two feet three inches apart. It is dropped in the drills by hand, in patches, each containing from twenty-five to thirty grains of seed, and about a foot from each other in the drill. The land is particularly clean, and the whole cultivation resembles more that of a garden than of a farm.

Every now and then we came to a farm-house. These are generally situated on the dry land at the lower sides of the hills, having the wooded hills behind them and the rice valleys in front. All had thatched roofs like the temples I have already noticed, although not built in such an expensive and substantial way. In almost every instance a species of iris was growing thickly on the flattened ridge of the roof, thus giving it a rural and not unpleasing appearance.

On the roadsides, and also in the little gardens of the farmers and cottagers, I frequently met with the tea-plant in cultivation. It was not cultivated largely in this part of the country, but, apparently, only in sufficient quantities to supply the wants of those around whose houses it was growing. Fruit trees of various kinds were common also on the lower sides of these hills, and, generally, in the vicinity of the villages. Pears, plums, oranges, peaches, chesnuts, loquats, Salisburia nuts, and *Diospyros kaki* are the most common fruit trees of this province.

The vine in this part of the country produces fruit of great excellence. The bunches are of a medium size, the berries of a brownish color, thinskinned, and the flavor is all that can be desired. This grape may be valued in England, where we have so many fine kinds, and most certainly will be highly prized in the United States of America. A few years ago I was travelling from Malta to Cairo, in company with William Cullen Bryant, the celebrated American poet, and a genuine lover ot horticultural pursuits. He informed me that, owing to some cause, our European vines did not succeed very well on the other side of the Atlantic, and suggested the importance of introducing varieties from China, where the climate, as regards extremes of heat and cold, is much like that of the United States. I had never met with what I consider a really good variety of grape in China, and therefore have not been able to act on Bryant's suggestion. At last, we had here a subject for the experiment; and I urged its importance on George Rogers Hall, of Yokohama, who is an American citizen, and who has already introduced a number of plants into his country from China, He entered warmly into the matter, and no doubt will accomplish the object in view.

The winter vegetables I saw were carrots, onions of several kinds, *gobō*, or Burdoch root (*Arctium lappa*), nelumbium roots, lily roots, turnips, ginger, *Scirpus tuberosus*, *Arum esculentum*, and yams.

Many of the forest trees of this district are identical with those found about Nagasaki, which I have already noticed. The largest and most useful seem to be such as *Pinus massoniana*, *Pinus densiflora*, *Abies firma*, *Reimospora pisifera*, *Reimospora obtusely*, and *Cryptomeria japordca*; the latter attains a very great size, and seems peculiarly at home. I have already mentioned *Thujopsis dolabrata* and *Sciadopitys verticillata*. The maiden hair tree (*Salisburia adiantifolia*) is common about all the temples and attains a great size. Here, as in China, the natives are very fond of its fruit, known in the Japanese shops by the name of *Ginko* or whitefruit. Evergreen oaks, of several species, are common in the woods over all this part of Japan. They attain a goodly size, and are most ornamental trees. Chestnuts of several kinds are also common; the leaves of one species (*Castania japonica*) are used to feed a kind of milkworm. Acers or maples are also common trees; many of the leaves of these are beautifully marked with various colors, and almost all of them take on deep colors as they ripen in the autumn, and produce a most beautiful and striking appearance on the landscape. But the already mentioned (*Ulmus keaki*) is perhaps the most valuable timber tree in Japan. It was introduced into Europe by Von Siebold some years ago, but I have not heard whether or not it is suitable to our English climate.

Amongst shrubs a species of Weigela was common, which at first I supposed to be the *W. japonica* of Carl Peter Thunberg, but it now proves to be *W. grandiflora*. It is covered with flowers during the summer months, and is really very ornamental. I also saw *Osmanthus aquifolium*, covered with sweet-scented white flowers. It belongs to *Oleaceae* (the olive tribe), and is a fine ornamental evergreen bush. In the gardens there is a variety with variegated leaves, looking somewhat like the variegated holly.

This is a charming shrub, and if it proves hardy in our climate will be a. great favorite. A new species of *Aucuba* not variegated like the one in English gardens, but having leaves of the deepest and most glossy green, was found common in the shady parts of the woods and hedges, and has now been introduced into England. As a fine evergreen bush it will be greatly prized; and, in addition to this, it produces a profusion of crimson berries nearly as large as olives, which hang on all the winter and spring, like the holly-berries of our own country.

One of my objects in visiting Japan was to procure the male variety of the common *Aucuba japonica* of our gardens. This is perhaps the most hardy and useful exotic evergreen shrub we possess. It lives uninjured through our coldest winters, and thrives better than anything else in the smoke of our large towns. Hence it is met with everywhere, and is one of the most common plants in the parks, squares, and houses of London. But no one in this country has ever seen it covered with a profusion of crimson berries, as it is met with in Japan. It belongs to a class of plants which have the male and female flowers produced on different individuals. Curiously enough, all the plants in Europe were females, and hence the absence of fruiting specimens. On my arrival in Japan, I lost no time in looking out for the male of this interesting species. I found it at last in the garden of Dr. Hall at Yokohama, who has also a very interesting collection of the plants of Japan, and to whom I am indebted for much valuable information and assistance. This plant was sent home in a Wardian case, and I am happy to say it reached England in good health, and is now in the nursery of Standish at Bagshot. I look forward with much interest to the eflfects of this introduction. Let my readers picture to themselves all the *aucubas* which decorate our windows and gardens, covered, during the winter and spring months, with a profusion of crimson berries. Such a result, and it is not an improbable one, would of itself be worth a journey all the way from England to Japan.

The geological formation of this part of the country differs entirely from that about Nagasaki. The latter bears a striking resemblance to the hilly part of China in the same latitude; that is, the upper sides of the hills are generally barren, with rocks of clay-slate and granite protruding in all directions. About Edo we meet with quite a different formation. (I have already described the substrata as exhibited by the sea-cliffs at Yokohama.) The country inland consists of hill and valley; and with the exception of the celebrated mountain named Fuji-*yama*, and some others in its vicinity, the hills are only a few hundred feet above sea level. The soil in the valleys, in which rice is the staple summer crop, is of a blackish-brown color, almost entirely composed of vegetable matter, and resembles what we meet with in a peat bog in England. Like that land it springs beneath the feet when one walks over it. The sloping sides of the hills are covered with trees and brushwood, the latter oftentimes being apparently of little value. Passing upwards through the belt of trees and brushwood, we next reach the tops of the hills. These are all comparatively flat, and thus a kind of table-land is the result. The soil of this table-land is exactly similar to that found in the marshy valleys below, that is, it is a soil closely resembling what is found in peat-bogs. Scarcely a stone or rock of any kind is seen, either in the valleys, on the hillsides, or on the table-land on the summits. A casual observer, on examining this black and apparently rich-looking soil, would think it very fertile, and capable of producing large crops; but in reality it is not so fertile as it looks, and foreigners generally remark on the little flavor the vegetables have that are grown on it.

How this peculiar formation was originally produced I am unable to explain. Whether this part of Japan was at some early period a flat peat-moss, and these hills formed by one of those fearful earthquakes for which the country is still famous, and which, according to tradition, forced up Fuji-*yama* in a single night to the height of more than 14,000 feet, I must leave to geologists to determine.

Visiting Edo

I gladly availed myself of an invitation from Consul-General Rutherford Alcock to visit Edo, and made preparations to start for that city on the 13th of November. On these occasions the stranger is always accompanied by mounted *yakunin* or government officers, who are in fact the police of the country. Their rank seems of a much higher grade than that of such persons in Europe, and they are treated with marked respect by all classes of the natives, who appear to stand greatly in awe of them. These officers are armed, each having two swords, and they are supposed to guard the foreigner in case of attack or insult by the way.

As we rode out of the courtyard of Loureira's house, I could not help smiling at the queer-looking individuals who came on behind me. Each of them wore a round, broad-brimmed straw hat and, as the day was wet, they had loose rain cloaks over their dresses. Their two swords, which were fixed in their belts at an angle of forty-five degrees, made their dresses stick out behind; and as we trotted or galloped along the road, they had a curious flyaway sort of appearance. As a general rule, they are but indifferent horsemen.

Our road—the Tōkaidō, or Imperial highway already mentioned—led us eastward, along the shores of the Bay of Edo. Small shops, teahouses, sheds for the accommodation of travellers, and gardens, lined each side of the way. Now and then we came to an open space with trees planted in the form of an avenue. These were chiefly of such species as *Cryptomeria japonica*, *Pinus massoniana*, *Celtis Orientalise* and *Ulmus keaki*. The glimpses I obtained from time to time through these trees and across the gardens behind them, were very beautiful. On the left, at a little distance, the view was bounded by some low hills of irregular form, crowned with trees and brushwood; while on the right the smooth waters of the Bay of Edo were spread out before us, here and there studded with the white sails of fishing boats.

The people along the road were perfectly civil and respectful. "*Ohaiyō*" or "Good morning" was a common salutation. Kaempfer informs us that in his time "multitudes of beggars crowded the roads in all parts of the empire, but particularly on the so much frequented Tōkaidō." Some of the members of Lord Elgin's embassy, if I remember right, seem to doubt the truth of this, as they did not meet with any on the occasion of their visit to Kawasaki; but on this occasion beggars were probably kept out of the way by the authorities. Truth compels me to state that at the present day, as in the days of Kaempfer, the beggars in Japan are numerous and importunate. As I rode along the road, there were many who sat by the wayside begging. These were "the maimed, the halt, the lame, and the blind," who, as I passed by, prostrated themselves on the ground and asked for alms.

Teahouses for the refreshment and accommodation of travellers formed the most remarkable feature on the road, and were met with at every few hundred yards. These buildings, like the shops, are perfectly open in front, and have the floors slightly raised and covered with mats, on which customers squatted and took refreshment. The cooking apparatus was always fully exposed to view, with its necessary appendages, such as pots, kettles, teacups, and basins. On approaching one of these teahouses some pretty young ladies met us in the middle of the road with a tray on which were placed sundry cups of tea of very good quality. This they begged us to partake of to refresh us and help us on our journey. When about six miles from Kanagawa we arrived at one of these teahouses which was rather larger than usual. Here it seemed to be the duty or privilege of the landlord to provide water for the horses of travellers and government officials, and consequently we found a man ready with a pail of water for our horses. It is customary to leave a small present in the coin of the country in return for these civilities.

With the exception of a few hundred yards here and there, the whole road from Kanagawa to Edo is lined on each side with houses. Now and then the single row expands into a village or town of considerable size, teeming with a dense population. One of these, named Kawasaki, stands about seven or eight miles east from Kanagawa. It seemed a busy market-town. The road forming the main street was lined with shops and teahouses, and crowded with people passing to and fro, buying and selling, or lolling about looking on. Travellers too were numerous, who were either going to the capital or returning from it on the great highway. Now and then we met a long train of coolies and armed men in the wake of a *norimono* containing an official or person of rank. The coolies were carrying the luggage, and the retainers were in attendance probably as much for show as for the protection of their master.

When we arrived at the farther end of Kawasaki we were again politely stopped by the host of the Hotel of Ten Thousand Centuries, a teahouse of the first class, who insisted on our entering his establishment for refreshment to ourselves and our good steeds. His invitation was seconded by three or four Japanese beauties, but we were ungallant enough this time to decline the hospitality, as it was unnecessary, and as these frequent stoppages were rather expensive.

At this place the Tama River intersects the main road. According to treaty, foreigners are not allowed to pass farther than this point in the direction of the capital, unless they belong to the legations of those nations who have treaties with Japan. Special permissions are however granted by the different ministers, with the sanction of the Japanese government. In all other directions from Kanagawa, except this one, foreigners are allowed to travel to the distance of ten *ri*, or about twenty-five miles. It will be seen, therefore, that there is a large tract of country available either for recreation or for researches in natural history, geology, and other sciences.

Dismounting from our horses, we crossed the Tama River in flat-bottomed boats, the horses being put into one, and the *yakunin* and myself going in another. This river is but a small stream of one hundred feet in width, and quite shallow. Our boats were guided and propelled across by long bamboo poles. When we had crossed the river we rode onwards in the direction of the capital. For some distance the road, the houses, and other objects, were just a repetition of what I have already described. After riding about two miles we arrived at a place called Omura, where there is a celebrated teahouse named Umeyashiki, which being interpreted means the Plum Tree Mansion. Here we were met by the host and some pretty damsels, and invited to partake of the usual refreshment.

The Umeyashiki is one of the best of the class to which it belongs. It is arranged in the usual style—that is, it has a number of apartments separated from each other by sliding doors, and raised floors covered with mats kept scrupulously clean, upon which the natives sit down to eat their meals and drink tea or *sake*. In front of the door there is a matted platform, raised about a foot from the ground and covered overhead. Ladies travelling in *norimono* or *kago*, when about to stop at the teahouse, are brought alongside of this platform, the bearers give the conveyance a tilt on one side, and the fair ones are emptied out upon the stage. They seem quite accustomed to this treatment, and immediately gather themselves up in the most coquettish way possible, and assume the squatting posture common in Japan.

Whether we really needed refreshment, or whether we could not resist the laughing-faced damsels above mentioned, is not of much moment to the general reader; one thing is certain, that somehow or other we found ourselves within the Umeyashiki, surrounded by pretty, goodhumored girls, and sipping a cup of fragrant tea. One lady, not particularly young, and whom I took for the hostess, had adorned herself by pulling out her eyebrows and blackening her teeth, which certainly in my opinion did not improve her appearance. However, there is no accounting for taste; and certainly our own taste, in many respects, is not so pure as to warrant us in throwing the first stone at the Japanese. The young girls who were in attendance upon me had shining white teeth, and their lips stained with a dark crimson dye. The Japanese innkeeper always secures the prettiest girls for his waiting maids, reminding me in this respect of our own publicans and their barmaids.

These inns and their waiting maids seem to have been much the same in the days of Kaempfer, in the year 1690, as I found them in 1860. "Nor must I forget," he says:

> to take notice of the numberless wenches the great and small inns, and the tea-booths and cook-shops, in villages and hamlets, are furnished withal. About noon, when they have done dressing and painting themselves, they make their appearance, standing under the

doors of the house, or sitting on the small gallery around it, whence, with a smiling countenance and good words, they invite the travelling troops that pass by to call in at their inn, preferable to others. In some places, where there are several inns standing near one another, they make, with their chattering and rattling, no inconsiderable noise, and prove not a little troublesome.

The Japanese ladies differ much from those of China in their manners and customs. It is etiquette with the latter to run away the moment they see the face of a foreigner; but the Japanese, on the contrary, do not show the slightest diffidence or fear of us. In these teahouses they come up with smiling faces, crowd around you, examine your clothes, and have even learnt to shake hands! Although in manners they are much more free than the Chinese, I am not aware they are a whit less moral than their shy sisters on the other side of the water.

In addition to tea, my fair waiting maids brought a tray containing cakes, sweetmeats of various kinds, and a number of hard-boiled eggs, which one of them kept cracking and peeling, and pressing upon me. As I was seated in the midst of my good-humored entertainers, the scene must have been highly amusing to a looker-on, and would, I doubt not, have made a capital photograph.

My *yakunin* were in a different room, and, apparently, had good appetites, and were making good use of their time. Leaving them to finish their meal, I took the opportunity of having a stroll through the large garden in front of the mansion. As its name implied, it contained a large number of flowering plum trees, planted in groups and in avenues. Little lakes or ponds of irregular and pleasing forms were in the centre of the garden, in which gold fish and tortoises were swimming about in perfect harmony. These little lakes were spanned by rustic bridges, and surrounded with artificial rockwork, in which ferns and dwarf shrubs were planted. Altogether the place was pretty and enjoyable, even at this time of the year. In spring or summer, when the trees are in full bloom, or covered with leaves, the Umeyashiki must be a charming place.

Bidding a polite adieu to our fair entertainers, we mounted our horses and continued our journey along the great highway. For the last three or four miles of the journey, the road had taken a direction more inland, and we had lost sight of the bay. Now the bay came again into view, and the road led along its banks as before. Gradually it became more crowded with people, the buildings and shops appeared of a better class, and everything indicated our near approach to the imperial city.

We now entered the suburb of Shinagawa, a place often mentioned in the writings of the Dutch travellers. On our left we observed many fine houses and temples, and some stately trees; while on our right the upper part of the bay lay spread out to our view. Before us lay the great city, encircling the head of the bay in the form of a crescent, and stretching away almost to the distant horizon. Far out in the bay a square-rigged vessel of war was lying at anchor; it proved to be the United States frigate *Niagara*, which had just brought home the Japanese ambassadors from their visit to America. A crowd of small trading vessels and fishing boats lay in the shallow water near the shore; and a chain of batteries commanded the anchorage.

While I was quietly observing all these objects, one of my *yakunin*, who was riding ahead to show the way, suddenly turned in to the left and intimated that we had arrived at the residence of the English minister. I found his Excellency at home; he received me most kindly, introduced me to the gentlemen of the embassy, and gave me quarters in the legation.

The British legation is located at the Tōzen temple, or rather in adjoining buildings, such as are attached to nearly all the large temples in Japan, and which are probably intended to receive visitors, or as seminaries for the Buddhist priesthood. It stands at the head of a little valley, backed behind and on each side by low richly-wooded hills, somewhat in the form of a horse-shoe, and open in front to. the Bay of Edo. The situation is exceedingly picturesque and beautiful. A fine wide avenue, some 200 yards in length, leads up from the bay to the residence of the English minister. Ornamental gateways stretch over the avenue and give it a pretty appearance, and here and there I observed some large examples of *Pinus Massonianay Cryptorneria japonica, Salisburia adiantifolia, Podocarpus macrophyllus*, camellias, &c.

On the west side of the temple there is a large cemetery covered with many thousands of stone tombs, some of them, apparently of great age. One of these cemeteries is attached to almost every temple about Edo, but this is the largest that came under my observation. They seem, in almost all instances, to be placed on the west side of the temples. The Japanese, like their neighbors in China, pay great attention to the graves of their dead. They frequently visit them, and place branches of *shikimi* (*Illicium anisatum*) or Japanese star anise and other evergreens in bamboo tubes in front of the stones. When these branches wither they remove them and replace them by others. The trade of collecting and selling these branches must be one of considerable magnitude in Japan; they are exposed, in large quantities, for sale in all the cities and villages; one is continually meeting with people carrying them in the streets; and they seem always fresh upon the graves, showing that they are frequently replaced.

A garden situated in the rear of the buildings of the legation, although small in extent, is one of the most charming little spots I ever beheld. The circular hill already noticed rises up behind, and forms a background to the picture: this hill is richly covered with trees of great size and beauty; particularly some fine evergreen oaks, seeds of which Alcock has sent to Kew. On the lower part of the hill there is some pretty rockwork covered with maples, azaleas, camellias, and other plants, with a species of plum, whose branches hung down like a weeping willow. At the base there is a small lake of irregular and pleasing form, extending the whole width of the garden, and between this and the temple there is a little lawn that gives a quiet and pleasing finish to the whole.

To complete the picture as it appeared to me: it was a bright autumnal day; an old maple tree with bloodred leaves was hanging over the lake at one end—an azalea, with leaves of a glowing crimson, was seen in groups at the other; patches of red, purple, and of almost every hue, met the eye in all directions, and produced a striking effect, backed as they were by the deep green of the camellia, evergreen oak, and pine. As the large trees in the background threw a shade over some parts of the garden, while the sun's rays streamed through other parts, or shone full upon the varied colors, the effect produced made one almost fancy oneself in some fairy land. Little walks led through amongst the bushes over the hillside, where the different plants can be minutely examined, and where shade can be had from the fierce rays of the sun. A fine avenue has been made on the top of the eastern spur, extending down towards the bay, from where a delightful view to seaward can be obtained, and where exercise and the cool morning and evening breezes can be enjoyed, without the nuisance of being followed by the officials of the Japanese government, an annoyance to which everyone has to submit if he moves out of the grounds of the temple.

The garden I have been describing is purely Japanese, Alcock having found it much in the same state as I saw it. The French consul-general, and his able secretary the Abbé Gerard, have each a garden, which they found attached to the temples given up to them as their places of residence. These gardens are all remarkable for azaleas of extraordinary size, which have been kept carefully clipped; and if they are covered with flowers in the spring, as I believe they are, they must be indeed charming objects to look upon.

The gardens and grounds of the legation are surrounded by a high wooden fence, and the gates are guarded by armed *yakunin*. If any of the members of the legation or their visitors pass out of this enclosure, they are immediately followed by some of these men. If the foreigner prefers a walk they walk after him; or if he goes out on horseback they follow in the same style. For some time this proceeding was thought to be quite unnecessary, and it was supposed that these men acted merely as spies, to report all the doings of the foreigners. The Japanese government have always maintained that it was necessary for our protection; and although it has no doubt signally failed in some instances, as for example, in the case of poor Heuskin the American interpreter, yet I have no doubt in my own mind that many lives have been saved by means of it. In so far as the government is concerned, I believe there is every desire to prevent disturbances with foreigners, and this is one of the means it uses to accomplish that object.

At the time of my visit there were an unusually large number of foreigners living in Edo. In addition to the members of the English, French, and American legations, whose countries had already made treaties with Japan, there was a deputation from Prussia engaged in making a treaty for that country, and a number of American officers who had come out in the *Niagara* with the Japanese ambassadors. Everything was going on quietly; and although a short time before Alcock's servant—a Japanese—had been murdered, and an attempt had been made upon the life of a Frenchman in the service of the French consul-general, the impression was that these men were probably not altogether blameless, and had brought such punishments on themselves. Be that as it may, no one seemed to have any hesitation in moving about, and I thus had an opportunity of seeing all the most remarkable parts of the city, as well as many suburban places of great interest. It is true that we were always followed by the guard of *yakunin*, but one had only to fancy himself a person of great importance—a *daimyō* or a noble in the far East—and this body-guard was easily endured. I found them always perfectly civil, and often of great use in showing me the right road.

An Assassination

On the day after my arrival in Edo Alcock was good enough to invite me to accompany him in a ride through some of the most interesting parts of the city. The legation is situated in the south-west suburb, and the main portion of the great city lies to the eastward from our starting point. There was nothing to indicate to a stranger the point where the western suburb ended and the city commenced; indeed, as it has been justly observed, the suburb of Shinagawa merges into Edo much in the same way as Kensington straggles into London.

Taking then an easterly course, a portion of our road led us through lanes fringed with fields and gardens, and through streets somewhat resembling those of a country town in England. During the first part of our route there was nothing particularly striking to attract our attention. Soon, however, we arrived at a spot of great interest. This was a little hill, one of the highest of the many hills which are dotted about all over the city. Its name was Atago-*yama*, which means the "Hill of the god Atago." On its summit there is a temple erected to the idol, and a number of arbores where visitors, who come either for worship or for pleasure, can be supplied with cups of tea.

Leaving our horses at the foot of the hill, we ascended it by a long flight of stone steps, which were laid from the base to the summit. When we arrived at the top of the steps, we found ourselves in front of the temple and its surrounding arbores. Here we were waited upon by blooming damsels, and invited to partake of sundry cups of hot tea. But the temple, the arbores, and even our fair waiting-maids, were for the time disregarded as we gazed upon the vast and beautiful city that lay below us spread out like a vast panorama. Until now I had formed no adequate idea of the size of the capital of Japan. Before leaving China I had heard stories of its great size, and of its population of two million; but I confess I had great doubts as to the truth of these reports, and thought it not improbable that, both as to size and population, the accounts of Edo might be much exaggerated. But now I looked upon the city with my own eyes, and they confirmed all that I had been previously told.

Looking back to the south-west over the wooded suburb of Shinagawa from which we had just come, and gradually and slowly carrying our eyes to the south and on to the east, we saw the fair city of Edo extending for many miles along the shores of the bay, in the form of a crescent or half-moon. It was a beautiful autumnal afternoon, and very pretty this queen of cities looked as she lay basking in the sun. The waters of the bay were smooth as glass, and were studded here and there with the white sails of fishing boats and other native craft; a few island batteries formed a breastwork for the protection of the town; and far away in the distance some hills were dimly seen on the opposite shores. Turning from the east towards the north, we looked over an immense valley covered with houses, temples, and gardens, and extending far away almost to the horizon. A wide river, spanned by four or five wooden bridges, ran through this part of the town and emptied itself into the bay.

On the opposite side of a valley, some two miles wide and densely covered with houses, we saw the palace of the *shōgun* and Daimyōkōji, the official quarter of the city, encircled with massive stone walls and deep moats. Outside of this there are miles of wide straight streets and long substantial barn-like buildings, which are the town residences of the feudal *daimyō* and their numerous retainers.

To the westward our view ranged over a vast extent of city, having in the background a chain of wooded hills, whose sloping sides were covered with houses, temples, and trees. A large and populous portion of Edo lies beyond these hills, but that was now hidden from our view.

Such is the appearance Edo presents when viewed from the summit of Atago-*yama*. This hill now bears the modern title of Grande Vue, and well it deserves the name. After we had enjoyed this magnificent view for some time, we descended by the stone steps and resumed our ride. Our road now skirted a hill clothed with noble timber trees and surrounded with walls. This was the imperial cemetery. A short distance beyond this we crossed the first or outer moat, and were then in Daimyōkōji, amongst the residences of the *daimyō* and their retainers. Here the streets are wide, straight, and cleanly kept, and altogether have quite a different appearance from those we had already passed through. Good drains are carried down each side to take off the superfluous water. All we saw of the houses of the *daimyō* was the outer walls, the grated windows, and the massive-looking doors, many of them decorated with the armorial bearings (*kamon*) of their owners. These buildings were low—generally two stories high; their foundations and lower walls were formed of massive stonework, and the upper part of wood and chunam. Judging from the general length of the outer street walls, the interior of these places must be of great size; indeed such must necessarily be the case, to enable them to accommodate the large number of retainers these *daimyō* always keep about them. As we rode along, many of these retainers showed themselves at the grated windows. It might be only fancy on my part, but I thought I could discern little good-will or friendly feeling towards ourselves in their countenances.

I have just stated that we crossed a bridge over a deep moat before entering Daimyōkōji, Edo's *daimyō* quarter. In order to give an idea of the plan of this part of the city, I may compare the moat to a rope loosely coiled; the end of the outer coil dipping as it were into the river, and supplying the whole with water. It is not correct to say, as is sometimes said, that there are three concentric circles, each surrounded by a moat. The *shōgun*'s palace and the offices of his ministers are situated in the centre of the coil, while the outer and wider portion encircles the mansions of the feudal *daimyō*.

The second or inner moat and enclosure was now in view in front of us, with its houses and palaces on rising ground. On the inner side of this circling-moat there are high walls on the water's edge formed of large blocks of stone, of a polygonal form, and nicely fitted into each other without the aid of lime or cement. This is a favorite mode of building in Japan in all cases in which stone is used. The plan is probably adopted in order to render such structures more secure in a country like this, which is so subject to earthquakes. In some places sloping banks of green turf rise steeply from the edge of the moat, and are crowned at the top with a massive wall. A landslip in these banks showed that the wall that apparently crowned their summits had its foundation far below, and that the banks themselves had been formed in front of the wall. On many of these green banks there are groups of juniper and pine trees, while inside the wall itself tall specimens of the same trees rear their lofty heads high above the ramparts. No embrasures or places for guns were observed in these walls, although one would imagine they had been erected for the purposes of defense. Kaempfer, however, assigns another reason; he says:

> Edo is not enclosed with a wall, no more than other towns in Japan, but cut through by many broad canals, with ramparts raised on both sides, and planted at the top with rows of trees, not so much for defense as ta prevent the fires—which happen here too frequently—from making too great a havoc.

A few months previous to the time of my visit, Ii Naosuke, the *tairō* or great elder of the empire, had been waylaid and murdered in open day, as he was proceeding from his residence to his office in the inner quarter. The scene of this tragedy was pointed out to me. A writer in the *Edinburgh Review* gives the following graphic account of this horrid murder:

> Within the second moated circle facing the bay, the causeway leads over a gentle acclivity, near the summit of which, lying a little backward, is an imposing gateway, flanked on either side with a range of buildings, which form the outer screens of large courtyards. Over the gates, in copper metal, is the crest of the noble owner—the chief of the house of Ikoraono in which is vested the hereditary office of regent, whenever a minor fills the *shōgun*'s throne. From the commanding position of this residence a view is obtained of a long sweep of the rampart; and midway the descent ends in a long level line of road. Just at this point, not 500 yards distant, is one of the three bridges across the moat, which leads into the inner enclosure, where the castle of the *shōgun* is situated. It was about ten o'clock in the morning of the 24th of March, while a storm of alternate sleet and

rain swept over the exposed road and open space, offering little inducement to mere idlers to be abroad, that a train was seen to emerge from the *tairō*'s residence. The appearance of the cortege was sufficient to tell those familiar with the habits and customs of the Japanese that the regent himself was in the midst, on his way to the palace, where his daily duties called him. Although the numbers were inconsiderable, and all the attendants were enveloped in their rain-proof cloaks of oiled paper, with great circular hats of basket or lacquered ware tied to their heads, yet the two standard-bearers bore aloft at the end of their spears the black tuft of feathers, distinctive of a *daimyō*, and always marking his presence. A small company of officers and personal attendants walk in front and round the foremost *norimono*, while a troop of inferior office-bearers follow, grooms with led horses, extra *norimono*-bearers, baggage-porters—for no officer, much less a *daimyō*, ever leaves his house without a train of baggage— empty or full, they are essential to his dignity. Then there are umbrel- la-bearers—the servants of the servants—along the line.

The cortage slowly wound its way down the hill, for the roads were wet and muddy even on the high ground, while the bearers were blinded by the drifting sleet, carefully excluded only from the *norimono* by closed screens. Thus suspended in a sort of cage, just large enough to permit a man to sit cross-legged, the principal personage proceeded on his way to the palace. Little, it would seem, did either he or his men dream of possible danger. How should they, indeed, on such a spot, and for so exalted a personage? No augur or soothsayer gave warning to beware of the Ides of March…The edge of the moat is gained. A still larger cortege of the *daimyō* of Kyushu, one of the royal brothers, was already on the bridge, and passing through the gate on the opposite side, while, coming up from the causeway, at a few paces distant, was the retinue of the second of these brothers, the *daimyō* of Owari. The *tairō* was thus between them at the foot of the bridge, on the open space formed by the making of a broad street, which debouches on the bridge. A few straggling groups, enveloped in their oil-paper cloaks, alone were near, when suddenly one of these seeming idlers flung himself across the line of march, immediately in front of the regent's *norimono*. The officers of his household, whose place is on each side of him, rushed forward at this unprecedented interruption— a fatal move, which had evidently been anticipated, for their place was instantly filled with armed men in coats of mail, who seemed to have sprung from the earth—a compact band of some eighteen or twenty men. With flashing swords and frightful yells, blows were struck at all around, the lightest of which severed men's hands from the poles of the *norimono*, and cut down those who did not fly. Deadly and brief was the struggle. The unhappy officers and attendants, thus taken by surprise, were hampered with their rain gear, and many fell before they could draw a sword to defend either themselves or their lord, A few seconds must have done the work, so more than one looker-on declared; and before any thought of rescue seemed to have come to the attendants and escorts of the two other *daimyō*, both very near (if, indeed, they were total strangers to what was passing), one of the band was seen to dash along the causeway with a gory trophy in his hand.

Many had fallen in the melee on both sides. Two of the assailants, who were badly wounded, finding escape impossible, it is said, stopped in their flight, and deliberately performed the *harakiri*, to the edification of their pursuers; for it seems to be the law (so sacred is the rite, or right, whichever may be the proper reading) that no one may be interrupted, even for the ends of justice. These are held to be sufficiently secured by the self-immolation of the criminal, however heinous the offense; and it is a privilege to be denied to no one entitled to wear two swords. Other accounts say that their companions, as a last act of friendship, despatched them to prevent their falling into the hands of the torturer.

Eight of the assailants were unaccounted for when all was over; and the remnant of the Regent's people, released from their deadly struggle, hurried to the *norimono* to see how it fared with their master in the brief interval, to find only a headless trunk. The bleeding trophy carried off had been the head of the *tairō* himself, hacked off on the spot. But strangest of all these startling incidents, it is further related that *two* heads were found missing, and that which was seen in the fugitive's hand was only a lure to the pursuing party, while the true trophy had been secreted on the person of another, and was thus successfully carried off. The decoy paid the penalty of his life. After leading the chase through a first gateway down the road, and dashing past the useless guard, he was finally overtaken; the end for which he had devoted himself having, however, as we have seen, been accomplished. Whether this be merely a popular version or the simple truth, it serves to prove what is believed to be a likely course of action; and how ready desperate men are to sacrifice their lives for an object. The officer in command of the guard, who allowed his post to be forced, was ordered the next day to perform the Harikari on the spot.

The rest of the story is soon told. All Edo was thrown into commotion. The ward gates were all closed; the whole machinery of the government in spies, police, and soldiers, was put in motion, and in a few days it was generally believed the whole of the eight missing were arrested, and in the hands of the torturer. What revelations were wrung from them, or whether they were enabled to resist the utmost strain that could be put upon their quivering flesh and nerve, remains shrouded in mystery.

Riding onwards, and keeping the citadel on our left, we passed two or three bridges that crossed the inner moat, and led into the palace and offices of the ministers. These personages and their servants may be seen daily going to office about nine or ten o'clock in the morning, and returning to their homes about four in the afternoon, much like what occurs at our own public offices. Some walk to office, some ride on horseback, and others go in *norimono*. Almost every man we met was armed with two swords. Now and then we met or passed a *daimyō*, or official of rank, accompanied by his train of retainers, armed with swords, spears, and matchlocks, and with the usual amount of luggage, large umbrellas, led horses, and other signs of his rank.

No foreign visitor to Edo is allowed to enter the sacred precincts of the inner enclosure we were now riding round. A short time before this, a portion of the palace of the *shōgun* had been burned down, and it was now being rebuilt. Judging from the part of it I saw in the distance, it did not seem a very imposing structure. Kaempfer writes in glowing terms of the palace of his day: " It had a tower many stories high, adorned with roofs and other curious ornaments, which make the whole castle look, at a distance, magnificent beyond expression, amazing the beholders, as do also the many other beautiful bended roofs, with gilt dragons at the top, which cover the rest of the buildings within the castle." As this work, however, professes only to give the reader a description of what came under my own observation, I must leave to others the description of the interior of the *shōgun*'s castle.

We had approached the citadel on the south, passed round it to the eastward, and were now on a rising ground on the north. Here another of those splendid views over the city and bay was obtained. This point has been named Belle Vue by foreigners, and deservedly so. It would be a mere repetition of what I saw from the Atago-*yama* to describe the scene which we now again beheld. Suffice it to say, that a vast city, bounded on one side by a beautiful bay, and on the other by the far off horizon, lay spread out beneath us. The land appeared studded all over with gardens; undulating ground and little hills were dotted about in every direction, crowned with evergreen trees, such as oaks and pines, and, although it was now far on in November, there was nothing to indicate the winter time in Edo.

The population of this fine city has been estimated at about two million souls. The extent of ground covered by Edo, and the main parts of its suburbs, has been stated by Kaempfer, on Japanese authority, to be about sixteen English miles long, twelve broad, and fifty in circumference. Judging from a native map of the city now before me, and from having ridden through it in all directions, I think the following is about its true size: From the southern suburb of Shinagawa to the north-eastern suburb the distance is about twelve miles, and from east to west it is about eight miles. Of course miles of extensive suburbs lie beyond these points, but these must be looked upon as being in the country and not in the town.

We could have lingered long on Mount Belle Vue, and gazed upon the beautiful panorama that lay before us; but the last rays of an autumnal sun reminded us that it was time to return home. Having completed the circle of the *shōgun*'s castle, we took a southerly course; and winding our way through streets that sometimes led us over little hills, sometimes through lanes and gardens, we in due time reached the gates of the British legation.

The Countryside

During my stay in Edo I made many excursions into the surrounding countryside—sometimes on horseback, and at other times on foot—but
invariably accompanied with a guard of *yakunin*. If the reader will accompany
me on one of these excursions, I shall endeavour to show him something
of the country, as I have already done of the town. Our road leads us
westward, and we are soon clear of the straggling suburb of Shinagawa. The
land is undulating in its general features, and consists of a succession of hills
and valleys. The valleys are low and flat, and capable of being irrigated by
the streams flowing down from the surrounding hills. Rice is the staple
crop of these low lands, and it was now of a yellow hue and ready for the
reaping hook of the farmer. The hills that encircle the valleys are covered
with brushwood and lofty trees. Here the gigantic *Cryptomeria japonica*, the
noble pine, and the evergreen oak are peculiarly at home. Clumps of
bamboos and the palm of the country (*Chamcerops excelsa*) give a sort of
tropical character to the scenery. The vivid hues of the autumnal foliage are
most striking, and produce a wonderful and beautiful effect upon the
landscape. The sumach and various species of maples have now put on their
varied shades of color—yellow, red, and purple; the leaves of the azalea
are changing into a deep, glowing crimson; and these masses of all hues
contrast well with the green foliage of the oaks and pines. As the eye wanders
over these valleys and hills, it rests at last on a conical mountain in the background, some 14,000 feet in height, and nearly covered with snow: this is
Fuji-*yama*, the holy mountain of Japan. It would certainly be difficult in all
the world to find a scene of greater natural beauty than this.

As we rode onwards we passed many snug little suburban residences, farmhouses, and cottages, having little gardens in front containing a few of the favorite flowering-plants of the country. A remarkable feature in the Japanese character is, that, even to the lowest classes, all have an inherent love for flowers, and find in the cultivation of a few pet plants an endless source of recreation and unalloyed pleasure. If this be one of the tests of a high state of civilization amongst a people, the lower orders amongst the Japanese come out in a most favorable light when contrasted with the same classes amongst ourselves. Vegetables, too, I saw in abundance. All foreigners who visit Japan remark on the little flavor possessed by the vegetables of the country. This is probably owing to the peaty nature of the soil. Although dark in color and apparently rich in vegetable matter, yet it has not the strength or substance of the soil which is found (for example) in the rich alluvial plain of the Yangtze River in China.

In one of the villages through which we passed we saw what appeared to be a family bathing room. The baths at the time were full' of persons of both sexes, old and young, apparently of three or four generations, and all were perfectly naked. This was a curious exhibition to a foreigner, but the reader must remember we are now in Japan. Bathing-houses or rooms, both public and private, are found in all parts of the Japanese empire—in the midst of crowded cities or, as we here see, in country villages. The bath is one of the institutions of the country; it is as indispensable to a Japanese as tea is to a Chinaman. In the afternoon, in the evening, and up to a late hour at night, the bath is in full operation. Those who can afford it have baths in their own houses for the use of themselves and their families; the poorer classes, for a very small sum, can enjoy themselves at the public baths. After coming in from a long journey, or when tired with the labors of the day, the Japanese consider a bath to be particularly refreshing and enjoyable; and it is probably on this account, as well as for cleanliness, that it is so universally employed. The stern moralist of Western countries will no doubt condemn the system of promiscuous bathing, as it is contrary to all his ideas of decency; on the other hand, there are those who tell us that the custom only shows simplicity and innocence such as that which existed in the Garden of Eden before the fall of man. All I can say is, that it is the custom of the country to bathe in this way, and that, if appealed to on the subject, the Japanese would probably tell us that many of the customs amongst ourselves—such, for example, as our mode of dressing and dancing—are much more likely to lead to immorality than bathing, and are not so useful nor so healthy. At any rate, the practice cannot be attributed to habits of primitive innocence in this case, as no people in the world , are more licentious in their behavior than the Japanese.

Never in my wanderings in any other country did I meet with such charming lanes as we passed through on this occasion. Sometimes they reminded me of what I had met with in some of the country districts of England; but I was compelled, notwithstanding early prejudices, to admit that nothing in England even could be compared to them. Large avenues and groves of pines, particularly of *Cryptomeria* were frequently met with, fringing the roads, and affording most delicious shade from the rays of the sun. Now and then magnificent hedges were served, composed sometimes of evergreen oaks of various species, sometimes of *Cryptomeria japonica* and other evergreens. These were kept carefully clipped, and in some instances they were trained to a great height, reminding one of those high hedges of holly or yew which may frequently be met with in the parks or gardens of our English nobility. Everywhere the cottages and farmhouses had a neat and clean appearance, such as I had never observed in any other part of the East. Frequently we came upon teahouses for the refreshment of travellers; and these had little gardens and fishponds in their rear, of which glimpses were obtained as we rode slowly by. The scene was always changing and always beautiful—hill and valley, broad roads and shaded lanes, houses and gardens, with a people industrious, but unoppressed with toil, and apparently happy and contented.

Such is the appearance of the sylvan scenery in the vicinity of Edo. I could scarcely fancy myself on the borders of one of the largest and most populous cities in the East, with a population of two millions of human beings, and covering nearly a hundred square miles of land. As we rode through this charming scenery, the stillness was broken only by the rustling of the leaves of the trees and the tread of our horses' feet. The people in the villages through which we passed were quiet and civil, and did not annoy us in any way. Little urchins sometimes shouted out *"Tōjin! Tōjin!"* as we passed by—

a term which means Chinaman, but probably is also used to designate a foreigner, or one who is not a native of Japan. I am not aware that the term is meant as an offensive one, and it certainly does not appear quite so bad as *Fan-kwei*, or *Pih-kwei*—that is, foreign devil, or white devil—terms applied to us in China rather too frequently. The dogs were the only animals that showed their enmity to us, and this they did in a manner not to be mistaken. They rushed out of the houses, and barked at us in the most furious manner; but they are cowardly withal, and generally keep at a prudent distance.

These dogs appear to be of the same breed as the common Chinese dog, and both have probably sprung originally from the same stock. It is curious that they should have the same antipathy to foreigners as their masters. For, however civil and even kind the natives of Japan and China appear to be, yet there is no doubt that nine-tenths of them hate and despise us. Apparently such feelings are born with them, and they really cannot help themselves.

That we are allowed to live and travel and trade in these countries is only because one class makes money out of us, and another and a larger one is afraid of our power. I fear we must come to the conclusion, however unwillingly, that these are the motives that keep Orientals on their good behavior, and force them to tolerate us amongst them. The poor dogs have the same feelings implanted in their nature, but they have not the same hypocrisy, and therefore their hate is visible. As watchdogs they are admirable, and that is almost the only use to which they are applied. Old Dutch writers inform us that these street dogs belong to no particular individual, but that they are denizens of particular streets—public property, as it were—and that they are regarded with a kind of superstitious feeling by the natives. They are "the only idlers in the country." I think these statements may be received as doubtful, or only partially true. Although some of these dogs may have neither home nor master, yet by far the greater portion have both; and if the inhabitants look upon them as sacred animals, and have any superstitious feelings regarding them, they certainly show these feelings of reverence in a peculiarly irreverent manner. On a warm summer afternoon these animals may be seen lying at full length in the public highway, apparently sound asleep; and it was not unusual for our attendants to kick and whip them out of our road in a most unceremonious way. On many of them the marks of the sharp swords of the *yakunin* were plainly visible; and everything tended to show that, if the dogs are regarded as sacred by some, the feeling fails to secure them from being cruelly ill-treated by the common people. It was not unusual to meet with wretched specimens in a half-starved condition, and covered with a loathsome disease. The fact that such animals were tolerated in the public streets almost leads one to believe that they must be regarded with superstitious feelings.

The lapdogs of the country are highly prized both by natives and by foreigners. They are small—some of them not more than nine or ten inches in length. They are remarkable for snub-noses and sunken eyes, and are certainly more curious than beautiful. They are carefully bred; they command high prices even amongst the Japanese; and are dwarfed, it is said, by the use of *sake*—a spirit to which their owners are particularly partial. Like those of the larger breed already noticed, they are remarkable for the intense hatred they bear to foreigners.

After a most pleasant excursion we found ourselves at the gates of the British legation, just as it was getting dark. The evenings were now cold, and some new stoves had been put up in the dining room. The first gong had sounded, and we were getting ready for dinner—a meal for which the excursion into the country had fully prepared us. But the day was not to end so agreeably as we had supposed. A pipe leading from the stove set fire to the roof of the dining room, and for some time it was feared the whole of the legation would be destroyed. The watchmen who surrounded the premises gave the first alarm to those outside by beating in a peculiar way upon the hollow stem of the bamboo. This emits a peculiar sound, which is heard a very long way off. Then the large fire bell sounded its alarm peal— a sound taken up by other bells, and repeated all over Edo. These fire-bells are established in all Japanese towns, and the custody of them is regularly organized. The manner in which they are tolled informs the people whether the fire is near or far off—whether they ought to come to render assistance at once, or hold themselves in readiness to come on a second warning. On the present occasion all the arrangements seemed to work most admirably. The gates round the legation were instantly closed and guarded by armed *yakunin*. The members of the fire brigade and those who had duties to perform were allowed to enter, but all others were strictly excluded. In a few minutes the place was full of armed men. Several hundreds were running about in all directions—in the garden, in the rooms, in the passages, and on the roofs of the different buildings; but watchful eyes were upon them everywhere, and not an article of any kind was stolen. The minister's table was covered with plate; his drawing-room contained numerous articles of interest and value, both native and foreign; yet, however tempting these things might have been, not a single article was missing. Altogether I had never seen such a perfect system of organization. In China it would have been a most difficult matter to have restrained the mob, who would have seized the opportunity to plunder; here it seemed perfectly easy, and everyone was under the most complete control. Scenes like this must be constantly happening in Edo. Fires are almost of daily occurrence in some part or other of the city; and owing to the houses being principally built of wood, the fires spread with great rapidity. The officers of the government and the members of the different fire-brigades have constant practice; and this, no doubt, accounts for their perfect system of organization, which was the admiration of everyone on the present occasion. Here, however, our eulogium must end.

The engines that were brought to put out the fire were the most wretched machines I ever saw. A little pond in the garden, in which there was a good supply of water, was not twenty yards from the house; yet the engine had to be filled with buckets by hand, there being no hose to connect it with the pond. The stream of water it threw out was little larger than that thrown by a hand syringe, and much less than could be discharged from a good garden engine. A number of men carried water in buckets up ladders to the roof of the building, and emptied it upon the flames; but here, strange to say, there was no system—no passing the buckets from hand to hand; every man was doing what was right in his own eyes; all were giving orders, and each one was making all the noise he could. Luckily the fire had been discovered early, and was easily extinguished, as the night was calm. Had it only got a little ahead before the discovery, or had a smart breeze been blowing at the time, the British legation in Edo, with the surrounding temples, would, in all probability, have been burned to the ground.

The fire was at last extinguished, but, ere this was accomplished, a con-siderable amount of damage had been done to the buildings. The rooms, papered in Japanese style, and divided from each other by moving panels, were strewed with charred wood, broken tiles, and deluged with water; the pretty garden was covered with rubbish, and several valuable plants hopelessly ruined. But in the midst of this we were all thankful that the flames had been subdued, and that we had still ample room in other quarters of the legation. And now the last scene of all took place, and a very sensible one it was. The high officers who had been superintending the fire brigade formed a kind of procession, and, with lanterns, marched up the ladders and over the roof, to judge for themselves and make sure that the flames were really extinguished. When everything was found in a satisfactory condition, orders were given for the people to leave, and in a few minutes the crowd of coolies, firemen, and two-sworded *yakunin*, had disappeared as quickly as they came.

A short time before I visited Japan, the English government had made the *shōgun* a present of a pretty little steam yacht that I am afraid will be of little use to His Majesty; and during my visit to Edo the government of the United States of America had presented to the Japanese all the newest and most destructive implements of war, and also had sent an officer over to instruct them how to use them. Should other nations in the West feel desirous of making presents, I would strongly recommend them to send out some good fire-engines, which would be of far more value to the Japanese than implements of destruction, which may one day be turned against the givers.

Gardens

The capital of Japan is remarkable for the large number of gardens in its suburbs where plants are cultivated for sale. The good people of Edo, like all highly civilized nations, are fond of flowers, and hence the demand for them is very great. The finest and most extensive of these gardens are situated in the north-eastern suburbs, at places called Dannozaka, Oji, and Sumaeya. As one of my chief objects in coming to Edo was to examine such places as these, I lost no time in paying them a visit.

As the British legation was situated in the south-west suburb, I had to cross the entire city before I could reach these gardens. From the time occupied in going this distance I estimated the width of the city, in this direction, at about nine or ten miles. Passing in from the western suburb, I went through Daimyōkōji, with its wide straight streets and town residences of the *daimyō* or lords and *daimyō* of the empire, which have been already noticed. On a rising ground on my left I saw the castle of the *shōgun*. Proceeding onward in an easterly direction, I recrossed the moat, and was again amongst the streets and shops of the common people. Here, on a hillside, in the midst of some tall pines and evergreen oaks, I observed a large building, which, I was informed, was a college for students of Chinese classics. A little further on I passed the palace of the *daimyō* of the Kaga domain, reputed to be the wealthiest and most powerful noble in the empire, and to have no less than 40,000 retainers located in his palaces in the capital, ready to do his bidding, whether that be to dethrone the *shōgun* or to take the life of a foreigner. He was reported to be at the head of the conservative party in the empire, and to be unfavorable to foreigners.

After passing the residence of the *daimyō* of Kaga, I found myself in the eastern suburb. One long street, with houses on each side of the way, and detached towns here and there, extended two or three miles beyond this. Turning out of this street to the right hand, I passed through some pretty shaded lanes, and in a few minutes more reached the romantic town of Dannozaka. This pretty place is situated in a valley, having wooded hills on either side, with gardens, fish ponds, and teahouses in the glen and on the sides of the hills. In the principal tea gardens the fishponds are stocked with different kinds of fish; and I observed a number of anglers amusing themselves fishing, in the usual way, with hooks baited with worms.

The most curious objects in this garden were imitation ladies made up out of the flowers of the chrysanthemum. Thousands of flowers were used for this purpose; and as these artificial beauties smiled upon the visitors out of the little alcoves and summer houses, the effect was oftentimes rather startling. The favorite flowering plum trees were planted in groups and avenues in all parts of the garden, while little lakes and islands of rockwork added to the general effect.

Having patronized this establishment by taking sundry cups of tea, I intimated to my attendant *yakunin* my intention to look out for some gardens of a different kind, in which I could purchase some new plants. But pleasure was the order of the day with them, and they coolly informed me there were no other places worth seeing here, and that we had better go on to the tea gardens of Oji. From information I had previously received, I knew they were deceiving me, and therefore proceeded to take a general survey on my own account. When they saw I was determined to look out for myself, they pretended to have received some information about other places, and said they were willing to guide me to them. Telling them I was greatly obliged, I desired them to lead the way.

A short walk to the top of the hill brought us to a long, straight, country-looking road, lined with neatly clipped hedges. Here I found a large number of nursery gardens, richly stocked with the ornamental plants of the country. Crowds of people followed us, and, although they were rather noisy, and anxious to see such a strange sight as a foreigner in these out of-the-way places, they were, upon the whole, particularly civil and easily managed and controlled.

As I entered a nursery, the gates were quietly closed upon the people, who waited patiently until I came out, and then they followed me on to the next. The *yakunin* seemed to be greatly respected, or feared it may be, but, at all events, a look, a word, or a movement of the fan, was quite sufficient to preserve the most perfect order.

I visited garden after garden in succession. Each was crowded with plants, some cultivated in pots and others in the open ground, many of which were entirely new to Europe, and of great interest and value. Every now and then my *yakunin* informed me that the garden I happened to be in at the time was the last one in the lane, but I told them goodhumoredly I would go on a little further and satisfy myself. This they could not object to, and, as more gardens were found, they only smiled and said they had been mis-informed. My old experience in China was of good service to me here. There is nothing like patience, politeness, and good humor, with these Orientals, whether they present themselves as noisy crowds or crafty officials.

At first the proprietors were not quite sure whether they ought to sell me the plants I selected, A reference was invariably made to the *yakunin*, both upon this point and also as to what sum they should ask. I am afraid I must confess to the impression that these gentry made me pay considerably more than the fair value or market price. As I concluded each purchase, the plants purchased, the price, and the name of the vendor, were carefully written down by one of the officials, and this report of my proceedings was taken home to their superiors.

The day was far spent before I had finished the inspection of these interesting gardens, but I was greatly pleased with the result. A great number of new shrubs and trees, many of them probably well suited for our English climate, had been purchased. Orders were now given to the different nurs-erymen to bring the plants to the English legation on the following day, and we parted mutually pleased with our bargains. It was now too late to go to Oji or Sumaeya, so that journey was put off until another day.

Mounting our horses, we left the pleasant and romantic lanes of Dannozaka and rode homewards. In coming out we had passed to the south of the *shōgun*'s palace, but in going home a different route was taken—a route that led us along the north-side of these buildings. In all my excursions about Edo with a guard of *yakunin*, I have invariably observed that they have brought me home by a different road from that by which I went. At first I gave them credit for a desire to show me as much of the city as possible, but I am now inclined to believe that they had orders of this kind from their superiors; and that the object was to prevent the chance of an attack from anyone who had seen us going out, and who might lie in wait for us on our return. Be that as it may, the fact is as I have stated.

On the following morning the whole of the nurserymen from whom I had purchased plants presented themselves at the British legation to deliver the plants and to receive their money—and possibly to pay a small tax to the officials. But if the latter transaction took place, it was done quietly and without a murmur.

A day or two after this, with a flask of wine slung over my shoulder, and a small loaf and jar of potted meat in my pocket, I started early in the morning in order to explore the country and gardens about Sumaeya and Oji. The same guard of *yakunin* accompanied me, and our road, for a good part of the way, was the same as that by which I went to Dannozaka. The places we now proposed to visit, although in the same direction, were considerably farther off. Passing, therefore, the scene of my former visit, I rode onwards farther out into the suburbs. The houses gradually began to get more scattered, sometimes fields and trees lined one side of the road, and everything showed me that I had fairly left the great city behind me. In one of these country parks I heard some soldiers going through their exercise; and the music was not unlike that of our own military bands. It was very likely an imitation of something of the kind. The high close paling and dense brushwood prevented me from seeing much, but sometimes I caught a glimpse of the flags and spears of the soldiers. The *daimyō* are constantly training their soldiers in all the arts of Japanese warfare. On this occasion, when passing near a *daimyō*'s residence in the city, I heard the clattering of arms, as of men engaged in fencing; and many times, during my stay in Edo, I have heard the same sounds. If ever any European nation has the misfortune to go to war with Japan, it will find the Japanese, as soldiers, very much superior to the Chinese. At the same time, as we do not fight with swords only, there is little doubt about the issue of such a contest. Let us hope that such a thing as a war with Japan may be far distant, and that, in this one instance at least, we may have the satisfaction of opening up a country without deluging it with the blood of its people.

Park-like scenery, trees and gardens, neatly clipped hedges, succeeded each other; and my attendant *yakunin* at length announced that we had arrived at the village of Sumaeya. The whole country here is covered with nursery gardens. One straight road, more than a mile in length, is lined with them. I have never seen, in any part of the world, such a large number of plants cultivated for sale. Each nursery covers three or four acres of land, is nicely kept, and contains thousands of plants, both in pots and in the open ground. As these nurseries are generally much alike in their features, a description of one will give a good idea of them all.

On entering the gateway there is a pretty little winding path leading up to the proprietor s house, which is usually situated near the centre of the garden. On each side of this walk are planted specimens of the hardy ornamental trees and shrubs of the country, many of which are dwarfed or clipped into round table forms. The beautiful little yew (*Taxus cuspidata*) I formerly introduced into Europe from China occupies a prominent place amongst dwarf shrubs. Then there aro the different species of pines, thujas, coniferous trees, and the beautiftd *Sciadopitys verticillata*, all duly represented.

Plants cultivated in pots are usually kept near the house of the nurseryman, or enclosed with a fence of bamboo-work. These are cultivated and arranged much in the same way as we do such things at home. The Japanese gardener has not yet brought glass-houses to his aid for the protection and cultivation of tender plants. Instead of this he uses sheds and rooms fitted with shelves, into which all the tender things are huddled together for shelter during the cold months of winter. Here I observed some South American plants, such as cacti, aloes, &c., which have found their way here, although as yet unknown in China—a fact that shows the enterprise of the Japanese in a favorable light. A pretty species of fuchsia was also observed amongst the other foreigners. In one garden I saw a large number of a species of acorus with deep green leaves. These were cultivated in fine square porcelain pots, and in each pot was a little rock of agate, crystal, or other rare stone, many of these representing the famous Fuji-

yama, the Matchless Mountain of Japan. All this little arrangement was shaded from bright sunshine and protected from storms by means of a matting stretched overhead. There was nothing else in this garden but the acorus above mentioned, but of this there must have been several hundred specimens. The pretty Nanking square porcelain pots, the masses of deep green foliage, and the quaint form and coloring of the little rocks, produced a novel and striking effect, which one does not meet with every day.

In Japan, as in China, dwarf plants (*bonsai*) are greatly esteemed; and the art of dwarfing has been brought to a high state of perfection. President Meylan, in the year 1826, saw a box he describes as only one inch square by three inches high, in which were actually growing and thriving a bamboo, a fir, and a plum tree, the latter being in full blossom. The price of this portable grove was 1200 Dutch gulden, or about 100£. In the gardens of Su-maeyah dwarf plants were fairly represented, although I did not meet with anything so very small and very expensive as that above mentioned. Pines, junipers, thujas, bamboos, cherry and plum trees, are generally the plants chosen for the purpose of dwarfing.

The art of dwarfing tree, as commonly practised both in China and Japan, is in reality very simple and easily understood. It is based upon one of the commonest principles of vegetable physiology. Anything that has a tendency to check or retard the flow of the sap in trees, also prevents, to a certain extent, the formation of wood and leaves. This may be done by grafting, by confining the roots in a small space, by withholding water, by bending the branches, and in a hundred other ways, which all proceed upon the same principle. This principle is perfectly understood by the Japanese, and they take advantage of it to make nature subject to this particular whim of theirs. They are said to select the smallest seeds from the smallest plants, which I think is not at all unlikely. I have frequently seen Chinese gardeners selecting suckers for this purpose from the plants of their gardens. Stunted varieties were generally chosen, particularly if they had the side branches opposite or regular, for much depends upon this; a one-sided dwarf tree is of no value in the eyes of the Chinese or Japanese. The main stem was then, in most cases, twisted in a zigzag form, which process checked the flow of the sap, and at the same time encouraged the production of side-branches at those parts of the stem where they were most desired. The pots in which they were planted were narrow and shallow, so that they held but a small quantity of soil compared with the wants of the plants, and no more water was given than was actually necessary to keep them alive. When new branches were in the act of formation they were tied down and twisted in various ways; the points of the leaders and strong-growing ones were generally nipped out, and every means were taken to discourage the production of young shoots possessing any degree of vigor. Nature generally struggles against this treatment for a while, until her powers seem to be in a great measure exhausted, when she quietly yields to the power of Art. The artist, however, must be ever on the watch; for should the roots of his plants get through the pots into the ground, or happen to receive a liberal supply of moisture, or should the young shoots be allowed to grow in their natural position for a time, the vigour of the plant, which has so long been lost, will be restored, and the fairest specimens of Oriental dwarfing destroyed. It is a curious fact that when plants, from any cause, become stunted or unhealthy, they almost invariably produce flowers and fruit, and thus endeavour to propagate and perpetuate their kind. This principle is of great value in dwarfing trees. Flowering trees—such, for example, as peaches and plums—produce their blossoms most profusely under the treatment I have described; and as they expend their energies in this way, they have little inclination to make vigorous growth.

The most remarkable feature in the nurseries of Sumaeya and Dannozaka is the large number of plants with variegated leaves. It is only a very few years since our taste in Europe led us to take an interest in and to admire those curious freaks of nature called variegated plants. For anything I know to the contrary, the Japanese have been cultivating this taste for a thousand years. The result is that they have in cultivation, in a variegated state, almost all the ornamental plants of the country, and many of these are strikingly handsome. Here is a list of a few to give some idea of the extent and number of these extraordinary products—pines, junipers, *Retinosporas*, *Podocarpus*, *Illiciums*, *Andromeda japonica*, *Euryas*, *Eleagnus*, *Pittosporum tobira*, *Euonymus* (yellow), aralia, laurus, and *Salisburia adiantifolia*. I have already said we must look upon the *Atuuba japonioa* of our gardens as only a variegated variety of that species. Then there is a variegated orchid! a variegated palm! a variegated camellia! and even the tea plant is duly represented in this happy family! The beautiful *Sciadopitys* verticillatay which is no doubt one of the finest conifers in Asia, has produced a variety which has goldenstriped leaves.

I was able to select a great number of new ornamental shrubs and trees that will one day, I hope, produce a striking and novel effect upon our English parks and pleasure grounds. Having settled the prices of the different plants selected, all the particulars were carefully written down by my attendant *yakunin*, as on a former occasion, and the vendors were requested to bring my purchases to the British legation on the following morning. We then took our departure for Oji.

Oji is the Richmond of Japan, and its celebrated teahouse is a sort of Star and Garter Hotel. Here the good citizens of Edo come out for a day's pleasure and recreation, and certainly it would be difficult to find a spot more lovely or more enjoyable. Our road led us down a little hill, and was lined on each side with pretty suburban residences, gardens, and hedgerows. On approaching the village crowds of people came out to look at the foreigner, although a species of that genus had not been particularly rare of late. Giving some of the boys our horses to hold, we were conducted to the interior of the teahouse, and attended by pretty, good-humored damsels. A small garden, with a running stream overhung with the branches of trees, green banks, and lovely flowers, was in the rear of the teahouse; and, taken as a whole, the place was extremely pretty and well worthy of being patronized by the pleasure-seekers of Edo.

Having partaken of the cakes, tea, hard-boiled eggs, and other delicacies set before me, I went out for a stroll in the surrounding country. As my *yakunin* were busy with their dinner, I tried to induce them to remain and finish it, telling them I was only going for a short walk, and that I would soon return. This they would not listen to, so I let them have their own way, and we all set out together. My chief object was to get upon the top of a hill in the vicinity, in order to have a good view of the country. A few minutes brought me to the top, which formed a kind of table-land, uncultivated, but having here and there a few groups of lofty trees. This forms the hunting grounds the *shōgun*. It is here that on certain occasions he watches the flight of the falcon in pursuit of the heron of Japan—a bird held sacred by the Japanese, and rigidly preserved by the authorities. There is also on this hill an archery ground for the *shōgun*'s soldiers, and a refectory for preparing a repast for his majesty's retinue.

The view from the top of this eminence was exceedingly fine. To the northward, a highly cultivated agricultural country lay spread out. It was the period of the rice-harvest, and the fields were now yellow with the ripening grain. The young crops of wheat and barley, already several inches above ground, were of the loveliest green, and contrasted well with the yellow ricefields. The country was well-wooded, and a little river was seen winding through the valley on its way to the head of the Edo bay. Taking the place as a whole, his majesty the *shōgun* could scarcely have found a more pleasant hunting-ground.

The day was now far advanced; indeed, my *yakunin* had been hinting some time before this that it was time to return to Edo. First, they looked to the heavens, and gravely informed me they thought it was going to rain; and when they saw this did not produce the desired effect, they told me evening was approaching, and that it was dangerous for me to be out after dark. This was no doubt quite true, and during my residence in Edo I invariably made it a rule to get back to the legation as soon after nightfall as possible. On the present occasion I intimated to them that I was now quite ready to return to the city, and we were soon on our way.

On our way back, and just when we were opposite to the residence of the *daimyō* of Kaga—whom I have already mentioned as unfavorable to foreigners—a drunken man was monopolizing the road, who, I was afraid, might give us some trouble. He had a long wooden pole in his hands, and was endeavoring to strike all who came in his path. One of my *bettō*, or grooms, was struck by him. But as the poor wretch could scarcely stand, it was very easy to get out of his way. He had no idea that a foreigner was behind him; and I shall never forget the peculiar wild and drunken stare he gave me when he observed me. Under the circumstances I judged it prudent to leave him in his trance of astonishment, and trotted onwards.

Intemperance in the use of ardent spirits is one of the vices of the Japanese. In this respect, if we can trust Thunberg, the Swedish physician, they must have degenerated sadly during the last hundred years. Amongst a long catalogue of their virtues, Thunberg says, they have "no play or coffee houses, no taverns nor alehouses, and consequently no consumption of coffee, chocolate, brandy, wine, or punch; no privileged soil, no waste lands, and not a single meadow; no national debt, no paper currency, no course of exchange, and no bankers (!)." It may have been so in Thunberg's time, although I confess to some doubts upon the subject; but it will be seen, from what came under my own observation, that things are very different now.

In these days it is a common saying that all Edo gets drunk after sunset! This is, of course, an exaggeration, but no doubt drunkenness prevails to a degree happily unknown in other countries at the present day. Even before the evening closes in, the faces of those one meets in the streets are suspiciously red, showing plainly enough that *sake* has been imbibed pretty freely. Nor is it in the capital city only that such a state of things exists. We learn from Pompe van Meerdervoort, the Dutch physician at Nagasaki, that one-half of the whole adult population are more or less inebriated with *sake* by nine o'clock every evening! When I state that a great proportion of these drunken people in the capital are armed with two rather sharp swords, and that in this condition they are often ill-natured and quarrelsome, it will be readily seen that the city of Edo is not a very safe place for foreigners to be about in after nightfall.

The remainder of our ride home from Oji was without any incident worth relating, and I arrived at the house of the English minister, well pleased with the successful issue of the day's excursion. On various occasions during my stay in Edo I repeated my visits to Dannozaka, Sumaeya, and Oji, and was thus enabled to add to my collections a very large number of the ornamental trees and shrubs of Japan.

To Edo Again

On the 23rd of November, I had an appointment with the Abbe Girard, who was formerly a missionary in the Ryūkyū Islands, and was now interpreter to M. de Bellecourt, the French consul-general, or chargé d'affaires in Japan. The Abbe, who was well acquainted with Edo, was good enough to offer to take me to some places of interest I had not yet seen. I found him residing in a little temple near the French legation, and well guarded with *yakunin*. He had in his house some rare specimens of Japanese singing birds, particularly one known to foreigners as the Japanese nightingale. This is a curious bird, if the stories which are told about its habits are true. It is said to inhabit the recesses of dark woods, and to shun the light of day. Hence in a domestic state it is usually kept in comparative darkness, a wooden box being dropped over its cage. This box has a small paper window, in order to admit a little subdued light. In this condition it sings charmingly, and has a full, clear, ringing note, wonderfully loud for so small a bird. The Japanese name of this little songster is *uguisu*.

After breakfast the Abbe and I mounted our horses and, accompanied by our two groups of *yakunin*, set out to visit the temple of Asakusa, which lies on the north-eastern side of Edo. Our route led us, not only through the portion of Daimyōkōji I had frequently visited, but also through the main streets of the trading part of the city. I confess I was rather disappointed. The streets were much wider and cleaner than those of the Chinese towns, but the contents of the shops appeared to be of little value. One must bear in mind that Edo is not a manufacturing or trading town in the usual sense in which the term is used. Hence, perhaps, I ought to have expected to see only the necessaries, or perhaps a few of the luxuries of life, exhibited in the shops here. Silk and cotton shops were numerous, and, if they did not obtain custom, it was not for want of the use of means. Men and boys were stationed in front of the doors trying all their arts to induce the passersby to go in and spend their money. Lacquer-ware, bronzes, and porcelain were exhibited in abundance, as were also umbrellas, pipes, toys, and paper made up into every conceivable article.

I may here mention in passing that Japanese paper is made chiefly out of the bark of the paper mulberry (*Broussonetia papyrifera*). It is particularly well suited for decorative purposes, such as the papering of rooms. It has a glossy, silky, and comfortable appearance, and many of the patterns are extremely chaste and pretty. The fan pattern, which looked as if fans had been thrown all over the surface, used to be much admired by foreign residents. For some reason it is made in very small sheets, which would render it rather inconvenient to our paper-hangers. This is no detriment in Japan, where labor is cheap. Japanese oil-paper is of a very superior quality, and is used for a variety of purposes. For a very small sum one can be clothed in a "Mackintosh" coat and trowsers capable of keeping out any amount of rain. As a wrapper to protect silk goods and other valuable fabrics from wet and damp it is invaluable, and owing to its great strength it is often used instead of a tin or lead casing. Despatch boxes, looking like leather, and very hard and durable, are also made of paper, and so are letter bags, purses, cigar cases, umbrellas, and many other articles in daily use. In addition to those purposes to which paper is applied in Western countries, in Japan it is used for windows instead of glass, for the partitions of rooms instead of lath and plaster, for fans and fan cases, for twine, and in a variety of other ways.

Articles used as food were displayed in abundance in all the streets of the commercial quarter. The vegetables and fruits of the country, such as I have named elsewhere, were in profusion everywhere, and apparently cheap. Edo Bay supplies the good people of Edo with excellent fish, and consequently the fishmonger was duly represented amongst the shopkeepers, where his wares could be purchased either dead or alive, fresh or salted. Butchers' shops were also observed as we rode along, showing that the Japanese do not live on vegetables and fish only. It is true that in these shops we did not observe any beef, for the Japanese do not kill their bullocks and eat them as we do; and, as the sheep is not found in the country, we, of course, could not see any mutton. Venison, however, was common, and monkeys were observed in several of the shops. I shall never forget the impression produced upon me when I saw the latter hanging up in front of a butcher's door. They were skinned, and had a most uncomfortable resemblance to the members of the human family. I dare say the Japanese consider the flesh of the monkey very savory; but there is no accounting for prejudices and tastes, and I must confess that I must have been very hungry indeed before I could have dined on these human-looking monkeys.

In our ride through town we noticed a large number of fire-proof houses, or godowns, for the protection of money or valuable goods in case of fire. These have thick walls of mud and stone, and are most useful in a country like this, where fires occur so frequently. Wooden watchtowers were also numerous in all parts of the city. These are posts of observation, from which a fire can be observed at a distance and an alarm given. Buckets of water were seen in every street, and frequently on the tops of the houses; and a kind of fire-police are continually on the watch by night and by day, ready to give instant notice and assistance.

After riding in an easterly direction for some time, we arrived at the celebrated Nihonbashi, or Bridge of Japan. This crosses a canal fed by a river a little to the south of the bridge, and which is apparently connected with the moat which encircles the official quarter and the castle of the *shōgun*. The bridge is a strong wooden structure resting on piles, and riveted together with massive clamps of iron. To a foreign eye there is nothing very remarkable in its appearance; but by the Japanese it is considered one of the wonders of Edo. From this bridge the distances to all parts of the empire are measured in *ri*; and hence it is usual to say, such a place is so many *ri* distant—not from Edo, but—from Nihonbashi. A *ri* is about equal to two and a half English miles.

A ride of about two hours brought us to Asakusa. Its massive temple was seen looming at the farther end of a broad avenue. An ornamental arch, or *torii*, was thrown across the avenue, which had a very good effect; a huge belfry stood on one side; and a number of large trees, such as pines and *Salisburia adiantifolia* surrounded the temple. Each side of the avenue was lined with shops and stalls, open in front like a bazaar, in which all sorts of Japanese things were exposed for sale. Toys of all kinds, such as humming tops, squeaking dolls with very large heads, puzzles, and pictures were numerous, and apparently in great demand. Looking glasses, tobacco pipes, common lacquerware, porcelain, and such like articles, were duly represented. Had the whole been covered over with glass, it would have been not unlike the Lowther Arcade in London. As we entered the avenue, we were followed by crowds of people, who had evidently seen few Europeans before; but although somewhat noisy, they treated us with the most perfect civility and respect.

On our arrival at the head of the avenue, we found ourselves in front of the huge temple, and ascended its massive steps. Its wide doors stood open; candles were burning on the altars, and priests were engaged in their devotions. It was the old story over again—unmeaning sounds, beating of drums, tinkling of bells, &c., which I had so often heard when a guest in the Buddhist temples of China.

The temple has numerous teahouses attached to it for the accommodation of visitors and devotees. Adjoining them are many pretty gardens with fishponds, ornamental bridges, artificial rockwork, and avenues of plum and cherry trees, which seem the favorite ones at all the teahouses and temples of Japan.

This place is most famed in the vicinity of Edo for the variety and beauty of its chrysanthemums. At the time of our visit they were in full bloom, and most certainly would have delighted the eyes of our English florists had they found themselves so far away from Hammersmith, the Temple, or Stoke Newington. I procured some extraordinary varieties, most peculiar in form and in coloring, and quite distinct from any of the kinds at present known in Europe. One had petals like long thick hairs, of a red color, but tipped with yellow, looking like the fringe of a shawl or curtain; another had broad white petals striped with red like a carnation or camellia; while others were remarkable for their great size and brilliant coloring. If I can succeed in introducing these varieties into Europe, they may create as great a change amongst chrysanthemums as my old protege the modest "Chusan daisy" did when she became the parent of the present race of pompones.

In order to make sure of getting the finest varieties, I decided to take suckers from those in bloom at the time of my visit, and further to take these same suckers home under my own care. Having settled the price with some difficulty, I then intimated to the proprietor that he should dig them up forthwith. To this he made many objections, not on his own account, but on mine. They would be inconvenient for me to carry, he said, and he was quite willing to dig them up next morning and bring them himself to the legation. I do not know that the man wanted to deceive me by bringing different and inferior kinds to those I had purchased, but I had been taken in once or twice in this way in China, and was determined not to be taken in again. I therefore expressed my best thanks for his good intentions towards me, but got him to let me have the suckers, to take home under my own charge.

The Japanese gardener understands the art of chrysanthemum culture rather better than we do, and produces blooms of wonderful size. This is done by great care, good soil, and by allowing only one or two blooms to be perfected at the end of a shoot.

The tea-plant was common in these gardens, and was frequently used as an edging for the walks. In this position it was kept clipped, and had a pretty and novel appearance. In other places in this district I noticed it was cultivated rather extensively for the sake of its leaves. There is also in the gardens of Asakusa a collection of living birds and other animals for the amusement of visitors who may happen to be fond of this branch of natural history. I observed green pigeons, speckled crows, a fine large eagle, gold and silver pheasants, mandarin ducks, rabbits, and squirrels amongst the collection. Altogether, there are many things here calculated to amuse and instruct the good people of Edo when they come out for a holyday; and when the plum and cherry trees are in blossom, these gardens must be very enjoyable.

Leaving Asakusa, with its temples, teagardens, and chrysanthemums, we returned up the avenue by which we came, and were again followed by crowds of wondering natives. Taking now a southerly direction, we came upon the Sumida River, a broad river that flows from the eastward, and empties itself into the bay of Edo. It is about as large as the Thames at Richmond or Kew. We crossed it by a wooden bridge, and then entered that part of the town called by the Japanese Kukō-*jima* or "Island Opposite to Edo." This is, in fact, the Southwark or Borough of the capital. It is large and densely populated; the streets run mostly at right angles with each other; and it is intersected by a number of wide canals.

Riding along the banks of the river, we soon found ourselves nearly clear of houses and in the country. As we looked back over the river, the city of Edo, with its temples, watchtowers, and undulating wooded hills, lay spread out before us, and formed a picture of striking beauty. Nearly all the land where we were was one vast garden; or to speak more correctly, it was covered with tea gardens and nurseries. There were hedges of single camellias (*Camellia sasanqua*) white and red, and China roses, all in full bloom, although it was now late in November. Many evergreen trees were there, clipped into fanciful shapes; and the indispensable flowering plums and cherries were in great abundance, although now leafless and in their wintry garb.

We paid a visit to a number of teahouses and gardens; and from the way in which they were arranged and planned, no doubt they are patronized by thousands during the spring and summer seasons, when picnic-loving and pleasure-seeking Edoites go out to enjoy themselves. Everywhere we were politely received, and tea pressed upon us by the proprietors of the gardens.

We were now some ten or twelve miles from the foreign legations, and declining day warned us to hasten our return. On our way back we followed for some distance the course of the river. There is a fine broad embankment all the way along the left bank, which we could not help contrasting with that which is now being formed at Pimlico and Chelsea. But the Edo embankment has probably been in existence for many generations—a monument to the foresight and enterprise of this extraordinary people.

In this part of Edo there is a celebrated Buddhist temple named Ekōin temple, which was erected to the memory of 180,000 human beings who lost their lives in one night about 160 years ago. As the story runs, on that night occurred one of those fearful earthquakes that so heavily afflict this beautiful country. Houses were thrown down in all directions, and hundreds were buried alive in the ruins; conflagrations naturally followed, and this city of wooden houses was almost destroyed.

Our attendant *yakunin* kindly offered to take us to this celebrated temple, which was only a very little out of our way on our route homewards. As we approached it I observed in front a statue of Buddha, and some upright stones carved with an inscription telling the visitor of the fearful catastrophe and where the victims were buried. When we ascended the stone steps in front of the temple, a noisy crowd followed and surrounded us; we being now in a part of the town densely populated, and seldom if ever visited by foreigners. In an instant we had the *yakunin* of the district in addition to our own by our sides, in order to protect us from insult or injury. Although noisy enough in all conscience, this crowd of people were good-humored, and, although naturally anxious to look upon such strange beings as we were considered to be, they were perfectly civil, making way for us in any direction we wished to go.

On entering the temple a curious scene was presented to our eyes. Candles were burning dimly on the altars, and incense filled the murky atmosphere with a heavy perfume. An old reverend-looking man occupied a kind of pulpit, and was engaged in a sermon or address to a number of young men, women, and children. This reverend gentleman and his youthful congregation had a part of the temple to themselves—a sort of chapel in fact, which was separated from the rest of the building by a network of string; not strong certainly, but perfectly sufficient for the purpose in this orderly country. On our entrance, followed by a noisy crowd, the preacher continued his discourse apparently as if he was perfectly unconscious of our presence. It was very different with the members of his congregation: all of them transferred their attention from the preacher to us; turning round, they fixed their eyes upon us, and commenced laughing and chatting in a manner that, if complimentary to us, certainly was not so to their reverend instructor. Not willing to annoy the old man, we did not prolong our visit in the temple, but left him to finish his discourse, and his youthful audience to profit by his teaching.

Earthquakes such as this temple and its monuments were designed to commemorate are fortunately rare even in Japan. In the days of the *Taikō-sama* Toyotomi Hideyoshi (about the year 1595), we are told that an earthquake of frightful violence took place. The sea rose to an extraordinary height, especially in the strait between Japan and Shikoku, attended with terrible destruction of life and property. In 1793 another terrible earthquake took place. "The summit of a high mountain in the province of Hizen, west of Shimabara, sunk entirely down. Boiling water rushed in torrents from all parts of the cavity, and a vapor like a thick smoke covered the mountain. Three weeks later, there was an eruption from a crater about half a league from the summit. The boiling lava flowed down in streams, and for many days the surrounding country was in flames. A month after, the whole island of Kyushu was shaken by an earthquake, felt principally in the neighborhood of Shimabara, It reduced that part of the province of Higo opposite to Shimabara to a deplorable condition; and even altered the whole line of coast, sinking many vessels that lay in the harbours. The last visitation of any great violence occurred in 1854. In Edo alone it is supposed that 200,000 human beings were killed at this time, partly by the falling buildings and partly by fires, which were raging in all parts of the city, occasioned by the earthquake. The little town of Shimoda, at the tip of the Izu Peninsulay, was laid in ruins at this time, and the Russian frigate *Diana* was wrecked in the harbour.

During my residence in Japan, earthquakes, although not of a violent character, were of frequent occurrence, and generally took place during the night. The sound of creaking timbers used to remind me of my experience in the cabin of a small steamer laboring in a heavy sea during or after a gale of wind. Then my bed used to move about in a most uneasy manner, as if some strong power was endeavoring to carry it bodily away, but, changing its mind, had set it down again. Bishop Smith, in his *Ten Weeks in Japan* gives an amusing account of his first experience of an earthquake. He says:

At 4 a.m. on the morning following my first night of sleeping in the legation, I was suddenly awoken by a loud rattling noise at my door, and a forcible lifting up of my bed, and its heavy descent with a violent jerk to the ground. I shouted again and again to no purpose, warning the supposed intruder from my room, and making it perceptible that I was on the alert. A continued shaking of the bed, and a rumbling noise throughout the building, at first suggested the suspicion that our native guards were right, and that I had to prepare myself for the irruption of some invader. The foe, however, came from a quarter which I little suspected. An English voice in a distant apartment exclaimed, "An earthquake!" The sign of panic amongst the native population was soon audible. The priests rushed to the temples and commenced reciting their Buddhist chants. The monks began their ringing of bells, and beating of drums and gongs at the neighboring shrines. The Japanese domestics fled into the open air, and for the moment all was confusion and dismay.

The natives of the country seem to dread these earthquakes even more than the foreigners who are now located amongst them. An intelligent Japanese, who spoke English well, expressed his fears that his country would one day disappear from the surface of the globe, and sink down under the waves of the ocean. He had been told that an island out at sea, once fair and verdant, covered with people and houses and trees, was now nowhere visible, and that ships sailed over the spot where it once was.

Earthquakes are so common in Japan, that meteorologists have a division in their tables in order to mark their occurrence. Charles Hepburn, to whom I am indebted for a table showing the temperature of Kanagawa, and which I shall have occasion to mention hereafter, has one of these columns in his table. By a reference to it, it will be found that from the 1st of November, 1859, to the 31st of October, 1860, no less than twenty-eight shocks had been felt. In November, 1861, four are marked, and in February, 1861, there are the same number. This will give some idea of the frequency of the shocks, and of the volcanic nature of the country. When we consider how often these earthquakes happen, and how awfully violent they sometimes are, it is scarcely to be wondered that the natives of the country view them with feelings of awe and dread, and express their fears that some day their fair and beautiful land may disappear in the sea.

As the Temple of Ekōin is situated in a part of the town rarely visited by foreigners, crowds of people came to see us take our departure. The police of the district escorted us beyond their boundary, and we were soon out of the crowd and trotting onwards through the principal streets of the town. On the way home I observed that our road was strewed with straw shoes that had been worn by men and horses. All the horses wear shoes of straw, which, when worn out, are replaced by others, the old ones being left on the road where they are cast off.

Back to Kanagawa

While engaged in making observations on the city of Edo and the country around it, I had been daily adding to my collections of new trees and shrubs. Now and then a bit of ancient lacquerware, or a good bronze, took my fancy, and was carefully put by. I frequently visited the gardens I have already described, and each time I discovered and brought away something new. John Gould Veitch,[1] the son of one of our London nurserymen, had also been in Edo, endeavoring to procure new plants for his father, and consequently our wants in this way were generally known amongst the people. Almost every morning, during my stay at the legation, collections of plants were brought for sale, and it was seldom that I did not find something amongst them of an ornamental or useful character that was new to our English gardens. This, of course, could not last for ever; and the time came when I had apparently exhausted the novelties in the capital of Japan. Baskets were now procured, in which the plants were carefully packed and sent down by boat to Yokohama, where Ward's cases were being made, in which they were to be planted and sent home to England.

On the 28th of November I left the hospitable quarters of the English minister, on my return to Kanagawa. I returned by the way I came—along the Tōkaidō, or great highway of Japan. Again we passed through the scenes I have already described: beggars on the wayside, mendicant priests, *bikuni* or begging nuns, travelling musicians, coolies carrying manure as in China, lumbering carts

1 John Gould Veitch (1839–1870), a great-grandson of John Veitch, the founder of the Veitch horticulture dynasty, was one of the first Victorian plant hunters to visit Japan.

and packhorses, and travellers of all ranks, were met and passed on the road.
Kaempfer gives us the following description of this religious order:

> They live under the protection of the nunneries at Kamakura f and
> Kyoto, to which they pay a certain sum every year, of what they get
> by begging, as an acknowledgment of their authority. They are, in my
> opinion, much the handsomest girls we saw in Japan. The daughters
> of poor parents, if they be handsome and agreeable, apply for and
> easily obtain this privilege of begging in the habit of nuns, knowing
> that beauty is one of the most persuasive incentives to generosity. The
> *yamabushi*, or begging mountain priests, frequently incorporate their
> own daughters with this religious order, and take their wives from
> among these *bikuni*. Some of them have been raised as courtesans,
> and, having served their time, buy the privilege of entering into this
> religious order, therein to spend the remainder of their youth and
> beauty. They live two or three together, and make an excursion every
> day a few miles from their dwelling house. They particularly watch
> people of fashion who travel in *norimono*, or in *kago*, or on horseback.
> As soon as they perceive somebody coming they draw near and address
> themselves, not all together, but singly, each one accosting a gentleman
> by herself, and singing a rural song; and if he proves very liberal and
> charitable, she will keep him company and divert him for hours…
> They wear a large hat to cover their faces, which are often painted,
> and to shelter themselves from the heat of the sun.

A number of shops, established for the sale of seashells, were observed
on the roadside, but they did not contain many species of interest. Dried
fruits for sale were numerous and plentiful, such as oranges, pears, gingko-
nuts (*Salisburia adiantifolia*), capsicums, chesnuts, and acorns. The fruit of
Gardenia radicans is used here as a yellow dye, in the same way as in China.
Amongst vegetables I noticed carrots, onions, turnips, Ulyroots, ginger,
gobbo (*Arctium gobbo*) nelumbiumroots, *Scirpus tuberosus,* arums, and yams.
Fish of excellent quality was exposed for sale in large quantities.

A little way out of Shinagawa my *yakunin* pointed out Suzugamori, the
place where criminals are executed. It is an uninviting-looking piece of ground

close by the highway. I find that Kaempfer notices the same spot as observed by the Dutch embassy upwards of two hundred years ago:

> A place of public execution, offering a show of human heads aryl bodies, some half putrefied and others half devoured—dogs, ravens, crows, and other ravenous beasts and birds, uniting to satisfy their appetites on these miserable remains.

On the present occasion I did not notice any of these revolting sights, and it is to be hoped that the Japanese have, like ourselves, become less addicted to judicial bloodshedding than they were at the time of Kaempfer's visit. It will be remembered that such exhibitions were not uncommon amongst Western nations at a later period even than that alluded to.

When we had crossed the Tama River we put up our horses at the inn of Ten Thousand Centuries, and proceeded on foot to visit the Kawasaki Taishi, a famous Buddhist temple situated about a mile and a half from the ferry. Our road led us through fields and gardens, all in a high state of cultivation. Rice appeared to be the staple summer crop of the low land of this district. Many gardens of pear trees were also seen on the roadside. The branches of these trees were trained horizontally when about five or six feet from the ground, sometimes singly in the shape of a round table, or in groups in the form of an arbour. The branches are supported by a rude trelliswork of wood. The pear of the district is a pretty round brown kind, good to look upon, but only fit for kitchen use. There are no fine melting pears in Japan; at least none came under my notice during my stay in the country. On the roadside there were many little shops in which tea and dried fruits were exposed to tempt the weary pilgrim on his way to worship at the temple. We also passed begging priests, ready to bestow prayers and blessings on the heads of those who gave them alms.

As we approached the sacred building, one of my *yakunin* ran before to announce our arrival. On entering the main gateway there was a tank of holy water on our right hand. All devotees, on entering, visits the holy well, and sprinkles himself with water before they enter the temple. For this privilege one pays a small sum, the amount expected being in accordance with the means of the giver. In most cases the poor give only a few cash of the country, about the value of a farthing of our money. My attendant *yakunin* did not fail to perform the ceremony like good Buddhists, after which we ascended the broad flight of steps leading up to the main hall of the temple. Many native visitors came in while we were there, and each one, reaching the door of the edifice, bowed low before its altars, and muttered some prayers. Inside there were a number of priests of the Buddhist faith, who had evidently an eye to the good things of this world, and who were busily engaged in selling books and pictures connected with the temple to the ignorant and superstitious who came to worship at its altars. The temple itself appeared to be a strong and massive structure. Huge paper lanterns were hanging from the roof, and a few Buddhist deities were observed on the altars. Otherwise it was not remarkable, and was far inferior to the chief temples commonly met with in China.

When we got back to the inn of Ten Thousand Centuries a number of the waiting maids of the place came running out to welcome us with the usual "*Ohayō*," or "Good morning; how do you do?" of the Japanese. I know that the main object of all this excessive civility is to bring custom to the establishment, and sundry *ichibu* out of the pockets of the traveller; but after all, there is much gratification in a kind reception, and it is not worth while to look too closely into the motives of those who give it. In the present instance we had a long walk over a dry hard road, the sun had been hot, and we were glad to accept the invitation given to us by the pretty damsels to enter the inn and refresh ourselves after our journey. The same scene was now exhibited as I have already described at the Umeyashiki. A low square table was placed before me, covered with different kinds of sweet cakes, dried fruits, and cups of tea. The young girls of the teahouse, kneeling in front and on each side of me, poured out my tea, and begged me to eat of the cakes and fruits, while one of them busied herself in taking the shells off some hard-boiled eggs, dipping them in salt, and putting them to my mouth. Surely all this was enough to satisfy and refresh the most weary traveller, and to send him on his way rejoicing.

But the best of friends must part at last, so I was obliged to bid adieu to the host and his fair maids of the Ten Thousand Centuries, and pursue my way to Kanagawa. Nothing particularly worthy of notice presented itself during the remainder of my journey. We met the same motley groups and queer-looking travellers on the highway; dogs barked, and children ran out of the houses to look at the foreigner, and to cry out, as loudly as their little lungs would permit, "*Anata, ohaiyō.*" The number of little girls, each having a child tied on her back, was one of the most amusing sights during our progress. As these ran hobbling along, and the little heads of the children bobbed about, in danger apparently of being shaken off, one could not help laughing. On reaching the temple in Kanagawa, in which my quarters were, my guard informed me that their presence was no longer necessary, and I was free again to roam about by myself in any direction I pleased. I must confess that, however highly honored I had felt during my visit to Edo, by having a mounted armed guard attending me wherever I went, yet the departure of the *yakunin* was a decided relief, and greatly did I enjoy a return to my former lowly estate.

John McDonald, of Her Majesty's legation in Edo, from whom I had received much kindness and assistance, had been good enough to forward my collection of plants in boats to Kanagawa, and these arrived in safety. My guide Tomi had been employed during my absence in making collections of seeds and plants; but I am bound to confess that, according to the accounts I received of his proceedings during my absence, it appeared his favorite *sake* had more attractions for him than natural history. As I had now secured living specimens and seeds of all the ornamental trees and shrubs of this part of Japan which I was likely to meet with at this season of the year, the whole were removed across the bay to Yokohama, and placed for safety in Dr. Hall's garden, until Ward's cases were ready for their reception.

The collection I had got together at this time was a most remarkable one. Never at any one time had I met with so many really fine plants, and they acquired additional value from the fact that a great portion of them were likely to prove suitable to our English climate. Amongst conifers there was the beautiful parasol fir (*Sciadopitys verticellata*), *Thujopsis dolabrata*, *Retinospora obtusa* and *pisifera*, *Nageia ovata*, several new pines and cypresses, and varieties of almost all these species having variegated leaves.

Amongst other shrubs there was a charming species of Eurya, having broad camellia-looking leaves, beautifully marked with white, orange, and rose colors; a pretty variegated Daphne; several species of privets, yews, hollies, box, and ferns. In addition to these there were two or three new species of Skimmia—shrubs that bear sweet-scented flowers, and become covered with red berries, like the holly, during winter and spring; a palm with variegated leaves, a noble species of oak, some new Weigelas, and a number of curious *chrysanthemums*.

This list of beautiful trees and shrubs, all new to English gardens, may appear a long one, yet I must add to it several representatives of other two genera particularly worthy of notice. The first is a shrub or small tree called *Omianthus aquifalius*. This genus is closely allied to the olive; it produces sweet-scented white flowers, and has dark-green prickly leaves like the holly. Curiously enough, the leaves on the upper branches and shoots of the *Osmanthus* are produced without spines, exactly as we see on old holly trees. All the species of *Osmanthus* have variegated varieties in Japan, many of which are very beautiful objects for garden decoration.

The other genus to which I would call attention is the well-known *Aucuba*. In Europe we know only the variegated variety of *Aucuba japonica* which is one of the most useful of our evergreens, inasmuch as it is perfectly hardy in our climate, and flourishes even in the smoke of large towns where our indigenous shrubs refuse to live. But in the shaded woods near the capital of Japan I saw the true species of *Aucuba japonica*, of which the variegated one of our gardens is, no doubt, only a variety. This species has beautiful shining leaves of the brightest green, and becomes covered, during the winter and spring months, with bunches of red berries, which give it a pretty appearance. In fact, the *Aucuba* of the woods near Edo is the Holly of Japan. I frequently saw hedges formed of this plant, which were very ornamental indeed. In the woods there are numerous varieties of both sexes, some of which show the faintest traces of variegation, while others are nearly as much marked as the *Aucubas* found in our English gardens. In addition to the *Aucubas* found in a wild state, I had, in this collection, several garden varieties, with distinct and beautiful variegation, and the male plant of our common garden species, to which I have alluded in an earlier chapter, the introduction of which is likely to add much to the beauty and interest of that useful shrub, inasmuch as we may now expect to have it covered, during winter and spring, with a profusion of crimson berries.

Many other species of interest might be named in the collection I had now got together, but the above will suffice to show how fruitful the field for selection had been in and near the capital of Japan. From the list I have given, no one will be surprised when he hears others tell of the lovely sylvan scenery of the Japanese islands. I have already endeavored to give a faint idea of such scenery; and it was now my intention to transfer to Europe and America examples of those trees and shrubs that produce such charming effects in the Japanese landscapes.

But the latter part of the business was no easy matter. To go from England to Japan was easy enough; to wander amongst those romantic valleys and undulating hills was pleasure unalloyed; to ransack the capital itself, although attended by an armed guard, was far from disagreeable; and to get together such a noble collection as I have just been describing was the most agreeable of all. The difficulty—the great difficulty—was to transport living plants from Edo Bay to the Thames, over stormy seas, for a distance of some 16,000 miles. But, thanks to my old friend Ward, even this difficulty can now be overcome by means of the well-known glass cases that bear his name. Ward's cases have been the means of enriching our parks and gardens with many beautiful exotics, which, but for this admirable invention, would never have been seen beyond those countries to which they are indigenous.

In a foreign country, however, even Ward's cases cannot be made without some difficulty. The carpenter contracted to make the framework of the cases would have nothing to do with the glazing, because he did not understand it. A Dutch carpenter, residing in Yokohama, undertook to do the glazing, but unfortunately broke his diamond and could not procure another to cut the glass! Luckily, however, these difficulties were got over at last, and a sufficient number of cases were got ready to enable me to carry the collection on to China. The steamship *England*, Captain Charles Dundas, being about to return to Shanghai, I availed myself of the opportunity to go over to that port with my collections, in order to ship them for England, there being as yet no means of sending them direct from Japan. Veitch had also put his plants on board the same vessel, so that the whole of the poop was lined with glass cases crammed full of the natural products of Japan. Never before had such an interesting and valuable collection of plants occupied the deck of any vessel, and most devoutly did we hope that our beloved plants might be favored with fair winds and smooth seas, and with as little salt water as possible—a mixture to which they are not at all partial, and which sadly disagrees with their constitutions.

The Inland Sea

On the 17th of December, 1860, the good steamship *England*, in which I was passenger, weighed anchor and proceeded to sea. The wind, which had been blowing a gale the day before, was now light and fair, so that we were able to crowd on all sail and made rapid progress. The headlands that had lately been christened Mandarin Bluff and Treaty Point,[1] were soon passed, and the pretty little towns of Yokohama and Kanagawa were lost to our view in the distance. In the afternoon we passed Cape Sagami and the volcanic islands at the entrance of the Bay of Edo, and were once more in the great Pacific Ocean, Cape Izu—that stormy cape, the dread of mariners, but which, I am bound to say, has as yet treated me kindly—was also passed, and then darkness set in, and the fair land of Japan was hidden from our view.

On the following morning I was up and on deck before sunrise, and was well rewarded by the beauty of the scene. Landward, Fuji-*yama*, or the Holy Mountain, was seen towering high above all the other land, covered with snow of the purest white, and its summit already basking in the rays of the morning sun, although that luminary had not yet shown himself to the denizens of our lower world. Sailors and passengers alike looked often and long upon that lovely mountain, and with regret we watched it gradually disappear from our view and sink below the horizon.

In the afternoon of this day we were abreast of Cape Ōshima, and soon afterwards entered the Kii Straits, which lies between the islands of Shikoku and the Ise Peninsula, and leads into the Inland Sea. A reference to the map

1 The Mandarin Bluff has since been bulldozed away, but survives as Honmoku City Park. Treaty Point is now the western landing point of the Tokyo Bay Aqua Line.

of Japan will give a better idea of the position of this sea than any description. No foreign vessel, except ships of war or transports, had been allowed to navigate its waters, and, as it had not been surveyed, it was necessary, in all cases, to obtain pilots from the Japanese government before attempting the passage. The *England* was not a ship of war nor in any way connected with the government, and, in ordinary cases, would not have been permitted to pass through the sacred waters of the Inland Sea. But as Captain Dundas and his passengers were all anxious to view the beautiful scenery of which they had often heard, a request was sent to the authorities for permission and pilots, backed by the following powerful reasons. Her Majesty the Queen of Great Britain had presented a handsome steam yacht to the *shōgun* of Japan, and the latter had made a selection of lacquerware, paper screens, swords, and a variety of other articles, to send to Her Majesty in return. Now, although the good ship *England* was not a man of war, and had no great warrior amongst her crew and passengers, yet she had on board the presents for the Queen, and on that account was surely entitled to all the honors of a ship of war. Besides, she might be wrecked if exposed to the stormy waters of the Pacific Ocean, the presents might be damaged or lost, and that was an additional reason why she ought to be allowed to take the smooth water passage. The propriety and prudence of the course suggested was perceived at once by the authorities, and pilots were granted forthwith.

As the night was calm and clear, we steamed onwards slowly, and found ourselves in the morning on the eastern side of the island of Awaji. There is a passage on the south-east side of this island, but at its centre is a dangerous whirlpool, which all mariners carefully avoid. We therefore took the northern passage. As daylight was breaking the ship got ashore on a bank of soft mud. Our Japanese pilots appeared to be steering right on to the island, thinking, no doubt, that the wonderful English vessel, that went along without sails or paddles, could pass over land and villages as easily as she could plough the waters of the deep sea. Without much difficulty we got the ship afloat again, and proceeded on our voyage, but our confidence in the knowledge of our pilots was considerably lessened. Going onward in a northwesterly direction, we approached the entrance to the bay of Hyōgo and Osaka.

This beautiful Inland Sea was greenish in color and smooth as a mill-pond. In the direction of the towns just mentioned it was studded with the white sails of small junks, showing that this portion of the Japanese islands must be densely populated. I saw fishing boats in all directions busily employed in securing food for the teeming population; and pleasant-looking villages and *daimyō* castles (of Akashi and Akō) scattered along the shores.

The town of Hyōgo, which is the seaport of the imperial city of Osaka, is one of the ports that, according to the treaty, should be opened to foreign trade in 1863; and from all accounts it is likely to prove the most important place in Japan. Kaempfer, who passed through Osaka about 170 years ago, tells us that he found it:

> extremely populous, and, if we can believe what the boasting Japanese tell us, can raise an army of eighty thousand men among its inhabitants. It is the best trading town in Japan, being extraordinarily well situated for carrying on commerce, both by land and water. This is the reason why it is so well inhabited by rich merchants, artificers, and manufacturers… Whatever tends to promote luxury, or to gratify sensual pleasures, may be had at as easy a rate here as anywhere, and for this reason the Japanese call Osaka the universal theatre of pleasures and diversions. Plays are to be seen daily, both in public and private houses; mountebanks, jugglers who can show artful tricks, and all the raree-show people who have either some uncommon or monstrous animal to exhibit, or animals taught to play tricks, gather there from all parts of the empire, being sure to get a better penny here than anywhere else.

In proof of this demand for luxuries in Osaka, Kaempfer tells us that:

The Dutch East India Company sent over from Batavia, as a present to the Emperor, a casuar, a large East India bird who would swallow stones and hot coals. This bird having had the ill luck not to please our rigid censors the governors of Nagasaki, and we having thereupon been ordered to send him back to Batavia, a rich Japanese assured us that, if he could have obtained leave to buy him, he would have willingly given a thousand taels for him, as being sure, within a year's time, to get double that money by showing him at Osaka.

Hyōgo and Osaka were visited by Alcock in the summer of 1861, and his dispatch to Earl Russell fully confirms Kaempfer's account:

> The approach to Hyōgo is good and easy, the anchorage secure; the navigation to Osaka for cargo boats short and easy also, not more than four or five miles from the bay, though some fifteen from Hyōgo, which is to Osaka what Kanagawa is to Edo. Only this last is a capital filled chiefly with *daimyō* and their retainers—dominant classes, which consume much and produce nothing, and are decidedly hostile to foreign commerce, as diminishing their own share and endangering its easy and secure appropriation; while Osaka is a great mercantile centre, situated on a plain intersected by twenty branches of a river, and spanned by innumerable bridges, some of them 300 paces across; with this great advantage (above all others) over Edo, that, although an imperial city, it is comparatively free from the two-sworded generation of locusts and obstructives. There are a large number of *daimyō* residences, occupying more than a league of the river's banks, but I fancy these are seldom occupied, or only temporarily, by their owners. Immense activity reigns everywhere; and although it was difficult to make much way in finding out the true prices, with *yakunin* whose business it was to mislead us and fill their own pockets, I saw enough to satisfy myself that, if anything like free interchange could once be established, this would supply a market more than equal in importance to all the other ports combined.

It would appear, therefore, that the towns of Hyōgo and Osaka are likely to be places of considerable importance in a mercantile point of view. In situation these towns possess great advantages. They are in the central and most populous part of the empire, are easily approached from the sea, and there is good anchorage for ships in Hyōgo Bay, or the Gulf of Osaka. Moreover, Osaka is only a day's journey from Kyoto, the residence of the emperor, and the sacred capital of Japan. Thunberg left Osaka by torchlight in the morning, and reached Kyoto the same evening. He says:

> Except in Holland, I never made so pleasant a journey as this with

regard to the beauty and delightful appearance of the country. Its population, too, and cultivation, exceed all expression. The whole country on both sides of us, as far as we could see, was nothing but a fertile field; and the whole of our long day's journey extended through villages, of which one began where the other ended.

These ports are not only placed in a most favorable position for commerce, but they also swarm with merchants; and they have few of those idle, two-sworded gentry, who are the curse of Edo, and who will render that capital unsafe as a residence for foreigners certainly during the lives of the present generation. The great tea-producing districts of Japan are also situated in this part of the country, a circumstance that will render these ports of considerable value to the foreign merchant. In fact, if we can rely upon the statements of Kaempfer, Thunberg, and other travellers— and their statements would seem to be confirmed in Alcock's despatch I just quoted—Osaka appears to be to Japan what Suzhou was to China in the days before the rebellion, and what it may one day become again— namely, the great emporium of trade and luxury.

As we were not at this time bound for Hyōgo or Osaka, we did not proceed further up the bay, but, bearing westward through a narrow strait between the islands of Awaji and Honshu, we soon reached a wider part of the Inland Sea. As we steamed along, the scenery was very lovely and enjoyable. A calm and glassy sea was skirted on each side by hills of various heights from 800 to 2000 feet, sometimes apparently rugged and barren, and sometimes covered with trees and brushwood. Thick clouds of morning mist rested here and there for a while amongst the hills and sometimes on the water, and then became dispersed, allowing us to view the charming scenery, which for a time had been obscured. Fishing boats were swarming in all directions, and their pretty white sails added not a little to the beauty of the scenery. The excitement experienced by the passengers, and even by the sailors, was something most unusual; sketchbooks, pencils, and journals were all in great request, and impressions were produced upon us all which will not easily be forgotten.

We were now in what is called the Harima-*nada*, or the Harima Sea. It gradually widens until the distance between the two shores—that is, between the islands of Japan and Shikoku—is about thirty miles. Our course lay nearer the southern than the northern side of the passage. In the afternoon we came to a group of islands, through which we sailed until the evening. Some of these are remarkable for their peculiar forms. One named Yoshima had a rocky summit, giving it the appearance of a huge camel kneeling to receive its load. Viewed from a different point, it looked like the ruins of an ancient castle. Another, nicknamed Chiisa-Fuji (Ōzuchi Island), or Little Mount Fuji, was a remarkable representation, although in miniature, of its snow-capped namesake. Both these islands will no doubt prove valuable landmarks to mariners in this sea, as they have probably been for ages past to the Japanese.

The scenery in this part of the sea was quite a panorama—ever shifting as we sailed onwards. Now we opened up a beautiful bay, with a fishing village on its shores, and terraced cultivation extending a short way up the side of the hills. Losing sight of this, other islands, bays, and coves came constantly into view to charm and delight the eye. In one flat valley on our left we had a good view of a town of considerable size, in which a *daimyō* of great power resided and reigned supreme. His castle (Marugame castle) appeared to be strongly fortified, and had numerous watchtowers on its walls. These castles are apparently numerous in all parts of the empire, for many of them were seen on the shores of the Inland Sea during our passage through it.

Although the scenery through which we had passed had been most picturesque and beautiful, yet the land did not appear to be rich or fertile. With the exception of little patches of terraced work near the seashore, the ground seemed in a state of nature where the hand of the agriculturist had never ventured to turn over the soil. Rocks, apparently of granite and clay-slate, with red barren earth, were seen everywhere in patches amongst the scanty vegetation of stunted fir trees. Perhaps in spring, or during the rainy season, when the hills are green, these islands may not present such a barren appearance; and no doubt, as in China, the interior may be rich and fertile, although the land is barren near the seashore. But though not rich in an agricultural point of view, the strange and romantic hills and valleys, the rugged rocks, and those sights of nature stern and wild, contrasted with towns and villages nestled in snug coves, and basking on the shores of this beautiful Inland Sea, made more than one of our little party express a wish to be set on shore, and to become a hermit of the glade for the remainder of his days amongst such scenery.

I was rather disappointed in the number of trading junks and fishing boats seen during the day. The weather was fine, and there was nothing to keep them in their anchorages near the shore had they really existed. A place like this in China would have swarmed with them; though, as I have already stated, they were numerous in the vicinity of the ports of Hyōgo and Osaka—towns which we know to he large and populous. This fact, together with the sterile character of the land, would lead to the conclusion that the western part of Honshu, and the northern part of Shikoku, do not possess a large population or an extensive trade. Time will show whether these surmises are correct, or whether this absence of marine traffic be due to some other cause.

There are numerous well-sheltered anchorages in many parts of this sea; but, as in China, there seem to be some special ones that only the natives are accustomed to use, to the total neglect of the others, and no doubt for native craft these are the best ones. We passed one of these favored places about three o'clock in the afternoon, and our pilot wanted the captain to go in there and anchor for the night. This proceeding did not suit the ideas of Englishmen, who are always in a hurry, and it was intimated to our good pilot that it was too early in the day to anchor, and that we must go on until the evening. Before dark another place was pointed out as a safe anchorage for the night. A fishing junk was at anchor a short distance ahead of us; and our pilot thought, naturally enough, that there must be good anchorage in her vicinity. But when we got up with the junk, a cast of the lead showed us that she was at anchor in a place where there were twenty-three fathoms of water! She had, no doubt, only a light kedge out, and had taken up that position for fishing operations. We therefore steamed onwards until our soundings gave twenty fathoms, when Captain Dundas, fearing to approach nearer the shore, dropped anchor for the night. A few minutes before we anchored the sun went down behind the islands of the west, and, in bidding the Inland Sea adieu for the day, lighted up the clouds in the most gorgeous manner, and gave them the appearance of mountains of fire and gold. And thus ended my first day in the Harima-*nada*.

Next morning, 20 December, at daylight, we weighed anchor with considerable difficulty, owing to the length of chain we had out in our deep anchorage. We discovered, too, that, at a short distance from where we had spent the night, there was an excellent anchorage, with only eight fathoms of water over it. During the forenoon we came up with a pretty-looking village of considerable size, named Ino-*shima*. Here the land appeared much more fertile than we had seen since entering the sea. The houses were scattered over the sides of the hills amongst fields and gardens of terraced land, and surrounded with healthy fruit trees, apparently pears. The young crops of wheat and barley were above ground, forming broad patches of the liveliest green, most pleasing to look upon. Halfway up the hills cultivation ceased and beyond all was barren or in a state of nature. One of our pilots informed us that he was a native of this place, and it was sketched immediately and romantically called "The Pilot's Home."

Our passage during the morning of this day had been straight and broad, and of easy navigation, even for a sailing vessel; but about 1 p.m. we entered a pass between some islands which was certainly not more than half a mile in width. Here the scenery was very remarkable, and perhaps the finest we had yet seen. Pretty villages, temples, and farmhouses were observed on every side of us. Now and then we passed a fertile valley, in a high state of cultivation, stretching far back amongst the hills. The houses, too, seemed to be nicely thatched and tiled, and had an air of comfort and cleanliness about them rarely seen in oriental countries. We appeared to be sailing down some smooth river, which every now and then widened or narrowed according to the formation of the land. Around us there were hills and mountains, of various heights and of every conceivable form. The lowest rose but a few feet above the water, while the highest seemed fully two thousand feet high. Here and there, in our progress, I observed a column of stone erected upon the top of a sunken rock to warn the mariner of the hidden danger. On one of the banks of this river-like sea a broad road was observed skirting the beach under an avenue of trees. Our pilots informed us that this was a portion of the Sanindō, or imperial highway, which leads all the way from Kyoto to Shimonoseki. Sometimes the sea appeared completely land-locked, and resembled a lake with its bays and inlets; at other times it had the river-like appearance I have already noticed. Some of us compared it to Loch Lomond, Loch Katrine, or the Kiles of Bute; but, although probably it had a partial resemblance to all these places in the Scottish Highlands, yet it had a character peculiarly its own.

In the afternoon we had a good view of the castle and fortress of Hiroshima, situated at the head of a deep bay. This castle is said to be remarkable in Japan for its great strength. It is supposed to be one of the strongest in the empire, and perfectly impregnable. A massive seawall was built along the seashore; while behind this wall were seen castles, turrets, and watchtowers, inhabited by this feudal chief and his numerous retainers. Leaving this bay and its stronghold on our right and to the westward, our course led us in a more southerly direction, the channel still narrow and winding. This part continued as populous as that which I have already noticed when we entered the narrows, and large villages, composed of comfortable-looking houses—not densely packed together, but divided by fields and gardens—were everywhere seen along the shores.

In the evening we passed out into a wider part of the sea, and anchored for the night at a place called Mitarai Bay. Boats in large numbers, filled with wondering natives, had been sculling round us to get a sight of the ship that went ahead without wind or sails, and of the strange beings from some far-off foreign land who crowded her deck. While we were sitting at dinner, and speaking of the strange and beautiful scenery through which we had passed during the day, a messenger came on board to inform us that the high officers of the place were coining off to pay us a visit. In a few minutes three quiet, modest-looking individuals were ushered into the cabin, and led up to the head of the table, where Captain Dundas was seated. They wanted to know whence we came, what we wanted, and whither we were bound—all of which questions, with many others, were answered to their entire satisfaction. They were politely offered wine, biscuits and sundry other things which were upon the table. Each of them tasted what was set before him, and then, pulling out a piece of paper, wrapped up in it the remainder of the solids, and thrust the parcel into his wide sleeve. Such is the custom of the country, and such is termed politeness in Japan. A numerous retinue of servants attended these high officials, all of whom were delighted with what was given to them, and begged for more! As these gentry took their departure, they intimated to us that an officer of yet higher rank than theirs was coming on board. This personage presented himself soon afterwards, and, giving his swords to an attendant, walked up to the head of the table as the others had done. The ceremony of questioning, drinking, eating, and pocketing was gone through a second time, and then, with many low bows and expressions of thanks, the great man and his attendants took their departure for the shore.

2 December we weighed anchor this morning as usual at dayhght. We were now in what is called the Suō-*nada*. It is wide, has few islands, and is connected with the Pacific Ocean by a wide passage known as the Bungo Strait. We were too far from the land to note anything worthy of interest on its shores. This sea is chiefly remarkable for gales of wind of great violence, owing, probably, to the Bungo Channel forming a sort of funnel between this Inland Sea and the Pacific Ocean. We were destined to experience one of these gales on the present occasion. It commenced in the morning, and by the afternoon had increased to a hurricane. The wind was not steady, but came down in fearful gusts, strong enough, almost, to blow anyone overboard who ventured on the poop of the vessel. A trysail, which had been set, was riven from the sheets, and its block shaken with fearful violence and thrown into the sea. The scene reminded me of a powerful bulldog tearing and shaking a cat, and then casting it away in anger when he had deprived it of life. In this state of things the *England* made but little headway, and it was decided that we should look out for a safe anchorage for the night. We therefore bore up for the mainland of Honshu, and made for a place called, in Japanese charts, Kaminoseki. This is a most extraordinary anchorage, and well worth the attention of those who navigate this sea. As we approached the land there seemed to be no shelter except an open bay, protected indeed by the land on the west, but fully exposed to the eastward. On nearing the shore we observed an opening on our left, not more than sixty yards wide, which looked at first sight almost artificial, but was merely natural nevertheless, and which led into a beautiful land-locked harbour. We steamed through this narrow passage, and anchored in thirteen fathoms water.

The place in which we now were had all the appearance of an inland lake, and was protected from the wind in all directions. On each side of us two small towns were observed, pleasantly situated on the banks of the lake, and forming little crescents along its shores. The houses had whitewashed walls, and appeared to be clean and comfortable looking buildings. Little temples also appeared on the hillsides, surrounded by pinetrees; and Buddhist priests were seen about the doors. Hills filled the background, well-wooded in some parts, and terraced in others all the way up to their summits, showing that here the soil was fertile and productive. *Pinus Massoniana* seemed to be the most common timber tree in this quarter. On our approach the whole of the inhabitants of these quiet and secluded villages came out of their houses to look at the strange *hifune*, or "fire ship;" but the water being rather rough, the wind tempestuous, and night closing in, none of them ventured off from the shore. This evening we were therefore allowed to dine in peace, and were not honored with the presence of *yakunin* and other high officers at our table.

Next day our progress was slow, as the gale was still blowing, and we anchored about eight o'clock in the evening. At daylight on the following morning the Strait of Shimonoseki, which leads out of the Inland Sea into the Sea of Japan, was visible ahead of us, and distant some ten or twelve miles. A large fleet of junks and boats was seen coming out from the strait, having, no doubt, taken shelter during the gale of the previous days. The entrance to this strait is about half a mile in width; it is bounded on the north by the western end of Honshu, and on the south by Kyushu. Two small towns, one on each side, were visible on ite shores. As we passed along, the strait widened considerably; and a large town, named Shimonoseki, was observed on our right hand. A little further on, to the left, the castle of the *daimyō* of Kokura was pointed out, and we met that worthy himself in a painted barge, going in the direction of Shimonoseki.

The scenery in the vicinity of the strait is hilly, the hills being often conical in form, and covered with trees and brushwood. Generally the country has that barren and uncultivated character I already often alluded to in describing our voyage down this sea. It presents a striking contrast to the volcanic regions near Edo, where every inch of land is capable of being profitably cultivated, although, for some reason, thousands of acres are lying waste, or covered with brushwood of little value. But although the shores of the Inland Sea—beautiful though they are—present a barren aspect to the voyager, yet there must be many rich valleys amongst these hills capable of producing abundant crops to supply the wants of man and beast. Glimpses of these were caught as we sailed along the shores, and there must have been many more hidden from our view. These streams flowing down from the mountains irrigate and fertilize, while the climate of Japan is probably one of the finest in the world.

Before we got clear of the strait some alarm was felt owing to the shallowness of the water, and it must be confessed we had no great confidence in the knowledge of our pilots. After having had for some time only three and three-and-a-half fathoms of water, we suddenly felt an unusual motion, which old sailors like myself knew to be an intimation from the ship that she was hard and fast ashore. And so it was; we had touched a bank having only two fathoms of water on it, which our good ship refused to go over, and from which she could not recede. Our Japanese pilots took the matter very coolly, and told us we should have to remain in our present position until the tide rose, when we should have water enough. This was all very well, and it turned out quite true; but what if one of those sudden gales for which this coast is famous had come on in the mean time! We had no fear for our lives, as we might easily have reached the shore in boats, but my beautiful collection of plants, which was on board, I certainly looked upon as being in the greatest danger. While matters looked rather gloomy, a goodnatured gentleman came up to me, and hoped my collections were insured!

Although the circumstances in which we were placed at this time were far from being pleasant, we could not resist having a good joke with two of our fellow-passengers. Dr. ——— and Mr. ——— had both been unfortunate at sea, and had related, during our voyage, the stories of their various shipwrecks. On more than one occasion they had been told that we held them responsible for any ill luck that might befall us during the present voyage; that both of them were evidently Jonahs; and that, if we chanced to get into danger, they must be prepared to go overboard in order to ensure the safety of the ship. When, therefore, all our efforts to get into deeper water appeared fruitless, and when the *England* began to bump uncomfortably on the ground, an intimation was conveyed to these gentlemen that their time had come, and that they had better prepare for the fatal plunge. The sacrifice, however, was not required, as the tide rose before we could carry out our benevolent intentions, and the vessel floated safely into deeper water.

As we had now passed out of the Inland Sea, Captain Dundas decided not to trust the native pilots any longer, and kept well out from all the dangers of the coast. It was now bitterly cold, and the tops of all the hills were covered with snow. We encountered another gale of wind when off the Gotō Islands, and reached the quiet little harbour of Nagasaki without any ftirther adventures, all of us highly pleased with our voyage through the Inland Sea. As the *England* remained three days at Nagasaki, I employed the time in visiting a number of places in the vicinity, and added several novelties to my collections. The face of the country had undergone a great change since my former visit. It was now winter; deciduous trees were leafless, the ricelands were lying fallow, and the hillsides were green with the young crops of wheat and barley. The dress of the people had changed with the season; and the children, instead of being carried on the backs of children as before, were now borne about on their bosoms.

As my Ward's cases were all quite full, it was necessary to pack the Nagasaki plants in baskets, and these were put away in the longboat on the starboard side of the ship. On the 29th of December we bade adieu, for the present, to the pleasant shores of Japan, and sailed for China. A short time after we had put to sea I felt some regret at not having put my plants in the boat on the port side, which, being to leeward, was less exposed to spray from the sea. It was lucky, as it turned out, that no alteration was made, for on the following day we encountered a heavy gale of wind; the ship rolled dreadfully; and a quantity of planks piled on the house in midships gave way, and carried the longboat, that hung on the port side, headlong into the sea! On the 2nd of January we arrived at Shanghai, where I was kindly received by Webb, the worthy successor of my old friend the late Beale.

My time was now fully occupied in repacking and preparing the plants for the long voyage yet before them. The most important portion was confided to the care of Captain Taylor, of the ship *Tung-yu*, who, a short time before this, had had the honor to introduce into Europe the living salamander now in the gardens of the Zoological Society of London. Captain Taylor delivered these plants in the most excellent condition. Some of them were exhibited before the Horticultural Society, at South Kensington, three days after their arrival in England; and it was remarked that they looked as if they had been luxuriating all their lives in the pure air of Bagshot in Surrey, instead of having just been landed from a sea voyage of sixteen thousand miles.

Return to Japan

In the spring of 1861 I returned to Japan, my object being to inspect the natural products of the country during the spring and summer months, as I had already done in the autumn and winter. The steamship *Scotland*, Captain Bell, in which I had taken my passage, was bound for Kanagawa, but called at Nagasaki on her way. The day of our arrival at Nagasaki was a holiday with the natives, and all were dressed up in their gayest clothing. One of the chief sources of amusement appeared to be kite-flying. In the air above the town, and all over the country, there was a swarm of paper kites, which I at first sight mistook for a flock of seagulls. The kites were generally of a diamond shape, and were painted in gay colors of red, white, and blue. In every street, on the house-tops, on the hillsides, and in the fields, there were numbers of both sexes and of all ages thus amusing themselves, and all seemed gay, contented, and happy.

There is a famous temple, named Daitoku-*ji*,[1] situated on the hillside above the town, which is well worth a notice. The view from this place, at the time of my visit, was extremely beautiful and full of interest. The whole town, the lake-like harbour, and the panorama of hills near and far off lay spread out before me. Many of the plum and cherry trees were now in full bloom. Most remarkable amongst them was a double-blossomed cherry, a variety producing bunches of flowers nearly as large as noisette roses. This is an ornamental tree of the first class. Being springtime (April 13th), many

1 The temple grounds of the Daitoku temple, which were situated at Chokushizaka, just east of Dejima Island, were popular among locals and tourists for the splendid view they offered of Nagasaki and its bay. Though the Daitoku-ji was dismantled in 1886, its grounds have since been turned into the Daitokuji Park. Due to high-rise buildings, the park no longer offers the view for which the site was once known.

other trees were bursting into flower; the leaves of all were freshly green; and, as the sun was shining brightly in a clear sky, the place was most enjoyable.

As the *Scotland* remained in the harbour for two days, I had an opportunity of taking an excursion into the country to note the condition of its agricultural products. The barley and wheat crops were now in ear, and would be fit for the sickle at the end of the month or the beginning of May. The cabbage-oil plant (*Brassica sinensis*) was now in full bloom, and filled the air with the fragrance of its yellow blossoms. These winter crops, when ripe, would be removed, and their places occupied by beans, sweet potatoes, melons, &c., the summer products of this part of Japan. Most of the low rice-lands had been lying fallow during the winter, but would soon be irrigated and prepared for this crop, which is the staple production in all parts of the East.

On the hillsides and in gardens numerous varieties of the azalea were in full bloom, but the largest garden-plants belong to the *Azalea vanegata* tribe, and these were not yet in flower. *Kerria japonica*, *Prunus sinensis* (single and double), camellias, and many other plants identical with those of China, were also covered with their pretty blossoms.

Many pleasant and agreeable days might have been spent at this time in Nagasaki, but it was necessary that the good ship *Scotland* should move on. As we passed out of the harbour, I could well have wished to steer north for the entrance to the Inland Sea, in order to feast my eyes once more on its wild and romantic scenery. But the *Scotland* had no Queen's presents on board, and as the outer passage, if not the most agreeable, was the safest in the present state of our knowledge, and the quickest, we steered in a southerly direction along the coast of Kyushu, for Van Diemen's Strait [Ōsumi Kaikyō]. This strait, with its peaked mountains and active volcanoes, has been noticed in a former chapter. It seems to be remarkable for the fearful storms that sweep through it from the Pacific Ocean. The first time I passed through we had a very heavy gale, and now, at about the same place, we were doomed to encounter another equally severe. In order to get a little shelter we made for the high land near Cape Chichakoff [Cape Sata]. This time I had the advantage of being in a steamer. As the coast is not well known, we did not make any attempt to find an anchorage, but steamed under the high land and then stopped the engines. A current carried us slowly eastward towards the Pacific, and the gale told us, in language not to be mistaken, whenever the ship had drifted beyond the shelter of the land. Whenever this was felt, steam was got up, and we moved back again under the shelter of the cape. For two days we were detained by this gale, now drifting outwards with the current and now steaming back for the shelter afforded by the land.

On the evening of the second day the gale moderated a little, and our captain decided to steam out into the waters of the North Pacific Ocean, where we spent anything but a pleasant night. During the next two days we were sailing up along the land, and passed the Bungo and Kino Straits, which lead into the Inland Sea. On the morning of the 19th we were abreast of Cape Tsumeki, inside of which is the Bay of Shimoda and the town of that name, so long the residence of Townsend Harris, the United States minister. The weather was now fine, the sea was smooth, and a considerable number of junks were passed sailing in the direction of Edo bay. Still, there was nothing on this coast like the busy, bustling scenes daily observed in fine weather on the coast of China. We must have more knowledge of the interior of the Japanese islands before we can say whether this is owing to the less populous condition of the country or to the habits of the people. The fact is as I have stated; the reason of such a difference will, no doubt, be explained in due time. In the afternoon we were opposite the islands near the entrance to Edo Bay, and the same night dropped our anchor abreast of the town of Yokohama. I left the ship on the following morning, and took up my residence on shore.

Besides timber trees and other ornamental plants suitable to our climate, and likely to prove valuable in England, I had decided to make a collection of various other objects of natural history, particularly insects and land-shells. With this view I had secured the services of Tunga, my old Chinese servant, and had brought him over with me from China to Japan. We were now out all day long, ransacking every valley and every hill for the objects we had in view. Tunga soon picked up a few words of the language of the country; and, as he was civil and inoffensive in all his ways, and carried a few cash in his pocket to reward those who assisted him, he grew very popular amongst the country people. When making collections of insects and shells in China, we always found it a matter of the first importance to enlist in our service the children about the cottages and farmhouses amongst the hills. In this way we were able to secure many specimens of great interest that never came under our own observation during the day. I therefore decided to pursue the same course with the Japanese. Some of my friends, to whom I mentioned my plans, informed me that such a system would not succeed in Japan, for that it had been already tried and had failed. Liberal rewards in money had been offered again and again, but the country people apparently did not want money, or, at all events, would not take the trouble to earn it. An experience of eighteen or nineteen years amongst Orientals led me to doubt the truth of the conclusion at which my friends had arrived. Human nature, I argued, must be much the same all over the East, if not all over the world; and what a little management with kindness and liberality could effect in China, might surely be accomplished in Japan.

With these principles to guide us, Tunga and I went to work in this new field and upon this virgin soil. We began by collecting for ourselves, and this excited no little wonder in the minds of the natives. Then we sat down in their houses, or in the verandahs at their doors, and showed them the treasures in our boxes. Having got into their good graces, we encouraged them to enter into our service by small presents of the copper cash of the country to show them that we were really in earnest, and that they would be paid for their exertions. I had several sketches of the rare *Damaster blaptoides*, which had been given to me by Stevens of Bloomsbury Street, London. These I distributed amongst them, and offered a liberal reward for each specimen of that remarkable insect. In this way we soon had hundreds of people of all ages enlisted in our service. The country round Yokohama was divided into districts; each district was visited at stated times, and, as we were seen approaching in the distance, the fact was telegraphed from village to village, and from hill to hill, by the clear, ringing voices of the children. The difficulty, if it ever existed, had been got over, and the Japanese proved to be as willing assistants in my researches as the Chinese had been.

While writing upon the subject of Japanese insects I take the liberty of quoting a letter published in the *Zoologist* for June, 1860, from my friend

Arthur Adams,[2] of Her Majesty's surveying ship *Actaeon* on the capture of *Damaster blaptoides* in Japan:

As I am in a good humor, having just fished up a new genus of mollusca from a pretty good depth, I will tell you at the risk of being tiresome all about it, as I am sure Adam White, at least, will be interested in the narrative.

I was walking solitarily—for all hands had gone on board to dinner—along the shell-strewn strand of Takashima, a jolly little island, not far from the shores of Nippon—walking along in a brown study, smoking a little clay cutty-pipe, and thinking chiefly of the contempt in which I should be held if some of my very particular friends saw me in this very disreputable rig, for my neck was bare, and my coat was an old blue serge, and as for my hat, it was brown felt, and, I must say, a shocking bad one. However, the sun was bright, the clear blue rippling sea was calm, the little island was clear and verdurous, and I smoked serenely. On a sudden my abstract downward gaze encountered a grotesque Coleopteron in a suit of black, stalking slowly and deliberately among the driftwood at my feet—stepping cautiously over the spillacan twigs, like a Catholic priest in a crowded thoroughfare. At once I knew my coleopterous friend to be *Damaster blaptoides*; for although my eyes are small, yet I have been assured by a young lady friend of mine—sometimes irreverently called Polly— that they are penetrating; and my friend Adam White, when he warned me not to forget my Carabs, had sent me a rough outline of the corpus of *Damaster*. So I carefully lifted my unresisting sable friend from his native soil, and. after giving him a good long stare, I deposited him in a bottle. From his name and appearances, I judge him to be cousin to *Blaps*, and I turned over the rockweed for his brothers and other relations; but though *Helops* was there, *Damaster* was not. Puzzled, but not baffled, I conceived his taste might be more particular, so I ascended the steep green sides of the island, and cast about for rotten trees; nor was I long in discovering a very promising stump, nicely

2 Arthur Adams (1820–78) was an English conchologist who traveled extensively in China and Manchuria, and Japan during a voyage in the Sea of Japan onboard HMS *Actaeon*.

decayed, and full of holes enough to captivate the heart of any beetle. Being, however, fatigued with my scansorial efforts, I sat down before the citadel of *Damaster*, and assisted my deliberations by smoking a solemn pipe. Having propitiated Nicotiana and matured my plan of operations, I commenced the work of destruction, when, lo! among the vegetable debris I descried a long dusky leg, anon two more, and then, buried among the ruins, the struggling *Damaster*. In this manner was the rarest beetle known captured by a wandering disciple of Aesculapius, and an eccentric Fellow of the Linnaean Society.

I had an opportunity of seeing a portion of Adams's treasures on board of the *Actaeon* in China. In addition to insects, he had a fine collection of seashells, which will prove of great interest to conchologists in Europe. His cabin was full of specimens illustrating the natural history of the different Oriental countries he had visited in the *Actaeon*.

This mode of fishing lasted for a few days only; the species in question appeared to come suddenly on the coast, and as suddenly to take its departure, first, however, leaving a good supply of its number to assist in feeding the inhabitants of Yokohama and Edo. It was a curious-looking animal, short, flabby, and blown up, looking as if it consisted chiefly of wind and blubber. Some of the natives said it was poisonous; but, if so, this could be only in certain conditions, for it was a great favorite with the Japanese, who cut it up, dried it in the sun, and preserved it for future use.

One morning towards the end of April I crossed the bay from Yokohama to Kanagawa, accompanied by Clarke, of the house of Dent and Co., established here. Our object was to visit some of the Buddhist temples in that part of the country, and to examine the vegetable products and other objects of interest by the way. Landing at Kanagawa, we crossed the long, narrow town, and soon found ourselves in the open country behind it. The first object attracting my attention was the change that had taken place in the appearance of the fields and the crops since I was last here. The low rice-lands, which had been lying fallow since the crop was gathered in November, were now being dug up, flooded with water, and manured. In China, bullocks and buffaloes are employed to plough the land; but in Japan it is prepared by manual labor alone: a pronged fork is employed to dig and break up the soil. Vegetable matter is used in a fresh state for manure, as in China. Women, old men, and children were employed on the edges of the fields, and on every hillside, in cutting grass and weeds for this purpose. These, being scattered over the land and mixed with mud and water, rot in a very short space of time and afford nourishment to the rice crops. A week or two after this fresh manure is thrown upon the land every trace of it disappears from the surface. It probably goes on decaying for some time underground, thus feeding in a peculiar manner the roots of the paddy with those gases given off during the process of decomposition. In the corners of many fields little patches of land had been carefully dug and manured as seedbeds for rearing the young paddy. Each of these patches was banked round with earth and connected with a mountain stream, so that it could be irrigated at pleasure. Some of these seedbeds had been already sown, and we observed the natives engaged in sowing others as we passed along.

On the dry hill-lands the crops of wheat and barley were coming into ear, beans and peas were in full bloom, the cabbage oil-plant (*Brassica sinensis*) here, as at Nagasaki, was seen in patches over the hillsides, and the air was perfumed with its fragrant blossoms.

All countries are beautiful in spring, but Japan is pre-eminently so. The trees were now clothed with leaves of the freshest green, and many of the early flowering kinds were in full blossom. On every hillside and in every cottage garden there was some object of attraction. The double-blossomed cherry trees and flowering peaches were most beautiful objects, loaded as they now were with flowers as large as little roses. Camellias, forming good-ly-sized trees, were common in the woods, and early azaleas adorned the hillsides with flowers of many hues. Here the *Azalea obtusa* with flowers of the most dazzling red, was peculiarly at home. I found this species some years ago in the gardens of China, but no doubt its native habitat is Japan, and it requires the bright sunlight of the East to bring out in perfection its brilliant color. *Cydonia japonica* was seen in a wild state, creeping amongst the grass, and covered with red blossoms; violets, often scentless, covered every bank; and several varieties of primrose (*Primula corticoides*) were met with under trees in the shady woods.

The Buddhist temples, always situated in the most charming positions, and having fine examples of the trees and shrubs of the country, full-grown and carefully protected, are objects of attraction at all seasons, but more particularly in spring. We visited many of these on our route; all of them were interesting, and none more so than Bugen-*ji*, a place I had visited when here in the autumn.

The Bugen-*ji* valley is a beautiful one; it leads up between two pretty green hills covered with brushwood, evergreen oaks, and pines. The same solemn stillness seemed to reign amongst the temples as I had observed on a former occasion, broken only at intervals by some priest, loudly rehearsing his prayers. At the principal entrance of this temple therfe are some large examples of the double-blossomed cherry tree. One of these was one mass of bloom, and very handsome it appeared. The broad cleanly-swept walk below it was covered with thousands of its petals, which were falling like thin flakes of snow.

On the 7th of May I left Yokohama, and crossed the bay to Kanagawa, where I took up my quarters at the large Shōbutsu temple which had been rented and fitted up by Messrs. Dent and Co.; but as they had removed their establishment to Yokohama, it was now unoccupied. Had I searched all Japan I could not have found a place better fitted for my pursuits. I had large rooms and verandahs in which I could prepare and store my collections of dried plants, seeds, insects, and shells, while the garden afforded ample space for the living plants I was daily adding to my stores, and hoped one day to. introduce into Europe. A Japanese porter, a gardener, Tunga, and myself, were the only occupants of this temple; and I must have had more confidence in the natives than perhaps was prudent, for my doors werenever locked, neither by night nor by day. Itinerant florists and nurserymen were amongst my daily visitors, and rarely arrived without bringing me something I gladly bought and transferred to my temple garden.

About the middle of May the now well-known Pavlownia imperialis was in full bloom in the grounds of a temple adjoining that in which I was located. Here it forms a tree about thirty feet in height; the stem is generally bare, but branches out at the top, and each branch terminates in a spike of large, lilac, foxglove-like flowers. The varieties of pinks are numerous and beautiful in this part of Japan, and they also were in bloom about this time. They are remarkable for their large blossoms of various hues, some being of the most briUiant red and scarlet, while others are colored much like our own. The finest poppies I ever saw were in gardens adjoining the imperial highway. The Japanese do not smoke opium like their firiends in China, but I beheve the seeds of the poppy are largely used by them for medicinal purposes. The double-flowering kinds have blossoms of great size, of many different colors, and are highly ornamental.

But the plant remarkable above all others I saw at this time, for its great beauty, was a new primrose (*Primula japonica*). I shall never forget the morning on which a basketful of this charming plant was first brought to my door. Its flowers, of a rich magenta color, were arranged in tiers, one above another, on a spike nearly two feet in height. It was beyond all question the most beautiful species of the genus to which it belongs, and will, I doubt not henceforth take its place as the Queen of Primroses.

Revisiting Edo

Having ransacked the oountry in the vicinity of Yokohama and Kanagawa, I was very desirous of paying another visit to the capital. The nursery gardens of Sumaeya and Dannozaka, in which I had found so many new plants during the previous winter, had no doubt many others of interest which could only be judged of in spring or early summer; but Edo was a sealed city to all who were not officials, unless they were specially invited as guests by their minister at the court of the *shōgun*. Unfortunately Consul-General Alcock, to whom I had been indebted for much kindness and hospitality on a former occasion, was now absent in China, and it was generally reported that no Englishman would be allowed to visit the city until he returned. Under these circumstances I was unwilling to make an application to the gentleman who had been left in charge of the legation, as he might not have the power to grant me my request, and at the same time it would be disagreeable, I thought, for him to refuse. What was then to be done? Alcock was not expected back until the end of June, and if I could not visit Edo until that time all the spring-flowers would be past, and the opportunity of adding some plants of interest and value to my collection would be lost.

Most anxious to accomplish the object I had in view, I wrote to Townsend Harris, the United States minister, and asked him to receive me for a few days at the American legation. Harris sent me a very kind reply, inviting me to his house in Edo, and begging me to remain there as long as I pleased.

Thus far everything went well, and I was delighted with the opportunity which I was likely to have of adding to the number of those useful and beautiful trees and other plants I had discovered in Edo the winter before;

but the sequel will show that things were not destined to go on quite so smoothly as I had anticipated.

On the 20th of May Portman and a guard of *yakunin* were sent down to meet me at the Tama River. I had frequently heard of a beautiful inland road from Kanagawa to Edo; and as I had seen quite enough of the Tokaidō, we decided to take the new route. Before striking into the country we paid a visit to the celebrated teahouse at Omura, which I have formerly mentioned. The large garden attached to the Umeyashiki was now in great beauty. The trees were in full leaf, forming shady walks and avenues where travellers or visitors could shelter from the sun's rays, which were now becoming more powerful every day. The pretty waiting-maids brought us sundry cups of tea with different kinds of cake. Pleasant, very pleasant, was the Umeyashiki, but it was necessary to move on.

Leaving the Tōkaidō behind us, we took a bridle path that led us more inland, and soon afterwards we struck a broad country road, by which we journeyed onwards in the direction of the capital. On our way we called at a place called Noborito to see a large specimen of wisteria (*Glycine sinensis*), one of the lions in this part of the country. It was evidently a tree of great age. It measured, at three feet from the ground, seven feet in circumference, and covered a space of trelliswork sixty feet by one hundred and two feet. The trellis was about eight feet in height, and many thousands of the long racemes of the glycine hung down nearly halfway to the groimd. One of them, which I measured, was three feet six inches in length. The thousands of long, drooping, lilac racemes had a most extraordinary and beautifril appearance. People came from far and near to see the tree during the time it remained in bloom; and as it was in the garden of a public teahouse, it brought an extensive custom to the proprietor.

Tables and benches were arranged under its shade, which at the time of our visit were well occupied with travellers and visitors, all sipping and apparently enjoying the grateful and invigorating beverage. As the day was cloudless, and the sun's rays powerful, we were not slow to imitate the example they set before us, so we sipped our tea, smoked a cigar, and admired this beautiful specimen of the vegetable kingdom.

Our road during the remainder of the journey was a very pleasant one, and led us through lanes fringed on each side with pretty hedges and tall trees, the latter affording a pleasing shade. Many little villages and comfortable-looking inns or teahouses we passed by the way. Most of these teahouses had gardens filled with pretty flowering plants for the enjoyment of their patrons, and in more than one of them we noticed a trellis covered with the wisteria in full bloom. This trailing tree is evidently a great favorite with the Japanese, and it well deserves to be so. Everywhere the people seemed most inoffensive and even friendly, showing a natural curiosity to see the *tōjin* (Chinamen or foreigners), as they called us, and now and then saluting us with the friendly "*Anata, Ohio.*" Japan would be a pleasant place to live or travel in were it freed from those bands of two-sworded idlers that infest the capital, and render a residence there sometimes far from agreeable.

As we entered the suburbs of Edo we met the young gentlemen of the English legation going out for a ride in the country, followed by a large number of *yakunin*. This was rather an unlucky meeting, as it afterwards turned out, although I had no idea at the time that I had done anything wrong. A few words were exchanged with those of them whom I knew, and we parted apparently good friends. Someone told me afterwards that Francis Myburgh, the only gentleman in the party unknown to me, and who it seems had been left in charge of Her Majesty's legation, looked very indignant; but as I did not observe his countenance, I was left in blissful ignorance of the wrath he was nursing to keep warm until some hours afterward.

We arrived at the American legation between five and six o'clock in the afternoon, where I was most kindly received by his Excellency. Like all the other foreign ministers in Edo, Harris occupies a large and roomy temple. An avenue leads up from one of the streets of the town to the temple. Two noble trees of ginko (*Saliaburia adiantifolia*) guard the entrance, and one of them is the largest specimen of the kind I have yet met with. Its circumference, about six feet from the ground, is twenty-eight feet, and it is fully a hundred feet in height. On one of the sides of this temple there is the usual cemetery, and behind it is a hill covered with lofty trees. Then there are the usual guardhouses filled with armed *yakunin*, and a small, quiet-looking place, which is said to be the residence of the *metsuke*, the spy or spies by whom the sayings and doings of everyone in the legation are duly chronicled.

While we were sitting at dinner this evening I received the following letter from Her Majesty's legation:

> A, no British subject can visit Edo without an invitation from, or the sanction of, Her Britannic Majesty's minister, or, in his absence, the officer in charge of Her Majesty's legation, from neither of whom you have received such invitation or sanction, I have to request you will take your departure from Edo without delay.
> I have, &c.,
> F. Or. Myburgh, In charge of H.B.M. legation.

Early on the following morning I sent a reply to this letter as follows:

> I had the honor to receive your letter of yesterday's date, upon which I beg to make the following observations, I returned to Japan a short time ago for the purpose of examining the natural products of the country during the spring months, hoping to make some discoveries that might prove useful at home. For this purpose it was of great importance that I should be able to visit the gardens about Edo. Unfortunately on my arrival at Kanagawa I found Her Majesty's minister absent from Edo, and I was given to understand that I could not obtain permission from the officer in charge of the legation to visit the city. His Excellency Alcock has always shown every disposition to forward my views, and had he been here I have no doubt he would willingly have granted the permission I required. Under the circumstances I wrote to his Excellency the American minister, and asked him to grant me that permission which I am sure I would have received from Her Majesty's representative had he been in Edo. Harris, in the kindest manner, invited me to his house as his guest, in order to enable me to accomplish the objects I had in view.
> With this explanation, I trust you will not insist on my leaving Edo for a few days, as it might be a matter of public regret should I be prevented from adding to our home collection some new trees or other plants of much interest.

Having despatched this letter, and trusting to receive a favorable reply, I was furnished with the usual guard of *yakunin*, and we rode out to visit the nursery gardens of Sumaeya and Dannozaka. We took the same route through the city I have fully described in an earlier chapter, and witnessed the same scenes. The Sumaeya gardens, however, presented quite a different appearance from what they had done in the autumn before. They had put on their summer dress; the trees were covered with leaves, and many flowering shrubs and herbaceous plants were in full bloom. Amongst those that interested me most, because they were new to me, were a beautiful new oak with large and handsome leaves, several new maples with leaves beautifully marked with rich colors, new species of weigela, clematis, lychnis, and a variety of Solomon's seal having its leaves beautifully striped with broad white lines.

The Dannozaka gardens, which were next visited, were ransacked in the same way. Every corner was examined, and several new and important plants which I had not seen by me during my former visits were added to my collections. I have already stated that the town of Dannozaka is in a valley, and very pretty it seemed, with its clean houses sheltered and adorned by richly wooded hills. It is a pretty place at all seasons, for there are so many pines and other trees that retain their leaves all winter, that the woods may be said to be evergreen. Now, however, the leaves and flowers of deciduous trees were mixed up with those of the evergreen oaks and pines, and formed a pleasing contrast.

As on former occasions, an account of all the plants I purchased and the sums to be paid for them was carefully written down by one of my attendant *yakunin*, and no doubt a full and particular report of my doings was forwarded to the proper quarter. This system has one great advantage, and it is this—the most perfect reliance may be placed on the men with whom you have made your bargains; they will certainly bring the articles at the time appointed, and will not attempt to demand more than the sum they have agreed to.

As these gardens were very numerous, the whole day was spent in examining them; and my attendants, long before I had finished, had been giving me sundry broad hints that it was time to set out on our return to Edo. When I had finished my investigations we mounted our horses and rode homewards, arriving at the American legation before nightfall. Here I found a letter waiting for me, of which the following is a true copy:

> I beg to acknowledge the receipt of your letter of today, and regret that you have placed me under the necessity of again writing to you. I care not to be informed now for what object you have come to Japan, or that Her Majesty's minister would have granted you permission to visit Edo had he been here—I only know that you are a private individual in a private capacity in this country, and that you have not asked for nor received the requisite sanction from the British authority here to come up to Edo.
>
> It is of no consequence to me now what you were given to understand at Kanagawa; but you must have been well aware that the American minister has not the power to grant you, or any other British subject, permission to visit Edo. It was your duty to have communicated with me on the subject, but this you had not the common courtesy to do; and you actually came up to Edo without even my knowledge. I think I have said enough to show you that you have acted in an improper manner. Whether it would be a matter of public regret or not your being unable to accomplish your private ends, is not a question for me to consider. I am only performing my public duty when I call upon you a second time to quit Edo at once. To allow you to remain would be to establish a dangerous precedent.
>
> I have, &c.,
> F. G. Myburgh

This communication did not take away my breath or my appetite for dinner, as, perhaps, it ought to have done. On the following morning (for I prefer to sleep upon anything disagreeable) I sent the following reply to the insulting letter I had received—a reply I trust will show that, although only a "private individual," I was incapable of doing anything rude or uncourteous:

> As I am unwilling to do anything that may have the slightest appearance of disrespect to Her Majesty's legation in Edo, I shall

leave the city at once—probably this evening, or, at latest, tomorrow morning. I may have been wrong in accepting the invitation of His Excellency the American minister without first obtaining permission from yourself (although, I believe, such a proceeding is not without a precedent), but I had no intention of, and could have no motive for, treating you with disrespect, as my letter of yesterday might have shown you. I have therefore to complain of the very uncourteous style of your last letter, which you have thought it your public duty to address to me as a British subject, and with this remark I beg to close my correspondence.

It is stipulated in the treaties the Japanese have made with foreign powers, that no foreigner, unless he be an official, can proceed nearer to Edo than that point where the Tama River intersects the Tōkaidō. But all the ministers who reside there had been in the habit of inviting their friends to Edo, apparently with the knowledge and sanction of the Japanese government. Even English ladies had been there on several occasions, and had returned highly delighted with their view of the great city. I had, therefore, no idea that I was committing a heinous offense in accepting the hospitality of the representative of a friendly power, particularly as it was well known I had no dangerous political objects in view. But I was unfortunately a British subject, and I had come to Edo (unwittingly, I must confess) without first bowing the knee to him who was dressed in a little brief authority. I have been travelling in Eastern countries for nearly eighteen years, and I can truly state that, during that long period, I have on every other occasion received the greatest and most disinterested kindness from every officer in Her Majesty's service with whom I have come in contact. I sincerely regret that I have had to mention one exception, which is perhaps not worth the prominence I have given to it in these pages. Let me turn, then, to a more agreeable subject.

On the morning after my visit to Sumaeya and Dannozaka the different nurserymen presented themselves at the American legation, with the plants I had purchased. Notwithstanding the shortness of the time I had been allowed to stay, the collection thus brought together was one of great interest, and mostly new to science. Orders were now given to prepare baskets to pack them in for conveyance to Kanagawa; and while these were being got ready, Harris invited me to accompany him in a ride into the country.

On our way we paid a visit to the grave of poor Henry Heuskens, formerly interpreter to the American legation, who had been waylaid and murdered by some Japanese a few months before. The tomb is placed in a quiet and beautiful spot on a hillside amongst some lofty trees. A neat and substantial monument, with a simple inscription, has been placed on the grave by Harris, and a hedge of evergreen oak and camellias has been planted around it on his orders.

Leaving poor Heusken's grave, we rode on in a westerly direction for about two hours, taking many a winding path in order to see the more remarkable portions of this beautiful suburban scenery, with which Harris was well acquainted, and of which he was one of the most enthusiastic admirers. Our destination was a place called Jūnishō *jinja*, or the shrine of the Twelve Altars. This shrine is situated in a wood, and has a waterfall on one side, and a lake on the other. Numerous teahouses do a thriving trade here, as the place is much resorted to by the good citizens of Edo. *Sake*, which is rather stronger than tea, is also consumed in considerable quantities. Report says that many of the visitors are particularly fond of composing and reciting poetry in one of the avenues near the shrine, and that sundry droughts of the favorite beverage are taken to brighten the intellect and to excite the imagination. At the upper end of this avenue there are sundry jets of water, each having a fall of about six feet, which are used in a curious way that is worth mentioning. It seems that, when the poet or philosopher, or whoever he may be, has imbibed so much *sake* as to render him incapable of further enjoyment—in fact, when he is what is vulgarly termed drunk—he gravely proceeds and places his head under one of these jets of cold water. This has the effect of making him a more sober, if not a wiser, man, and it enables him to return once more to the enjoyment of his *sake*. How often this system can be repeated in an afternoon with the same results, I am not informed. It is to be hoped that it is more beneficial to the literature of the country than it can be to the constitutions of those who thus enjoy themselves at the shrine of the Twelve Altars.

After visiting the waterfall. Poets' Avenue, and other places of interest, we sat down in one of the little sheds on the banks of the lake, and refreshed ourselves with sundry cups of hot tea. We returned home by a different road, and the same kinds of beautiful lanes, valleys, country houses, and gardens were passed as on our way out. A ride of some six miles brought us again to the great city, and we were soon threading our way amongst crowds of human beings, packhorses, and dust—a striking contrast to that sylvan scenery which we had just been enjoying.

Harris related an amusing circumstance connected to the shoeing of horses in Japan, which illustrates the ready way in which the people of the country adopt foreign customs when seen to be improvements on their own. I have already had occasion to mention the marked difference that exists between the Chinese and the Japanese in this respect. "*Oula custom*"— old custom—is the barrier to every foreign introduction in China, while the Japanese adopt, with promptness every improvement set before them. When Townsend Harris first went to reside in Edo, his horse was shod with iron shoes in the usual way. Up to this time the horses of the Japanese either wore straw shoes, or were not shod at all. One day an officer came to Harris and asked him to lend him his horse, and to be good enough to ask no questions as to the purpose for which the animal was required. This strange request was good-humoredly complied with, and the horse, after being away for a short time, was duly brought hack. The officer to whom it had been lent came to the American legation a few days afterwards, and told Harris, as a great secret, that the prime minister had sent for the horse to examine his shoes; and now, he said, the minister's horse had been shod in the same way, and all the horses of the other officers were likewise being shod!

As I did not wish to embroil myself in any way with the authorities of Her Majesty's legation, I left Edo on the following morning, and took the road to Kanagawa.

In this and in former chapters I have endeavored to give a description of the Japanese capital and suburbs, and I shall now end my account with a few general observations. Although Edo is a large city, and remarkable in many ways, it cannot be compared with London, Paris, or any of the chief towns in Europe, either in the architecture of its buildings, the magnificence of its shops, or in the value of its merchandize. It has no Woolwich or Greenwich—no St. Paul's or Westminster Abbey—no Champs Elysees or Versailles; it has nothing to show like the Boulevards in Paris or like Regent

Street in London. Indeed lite habits and wants of the people are so different from those of European nations, that we have little in common for a comparison. But Edo is nevertheless a wonderful place, and will always posess attractions peculiarly its own in the eyes of a foreign visitor. It is of great size for an Oriental city; its castle surrounded by deep moats and grassy banks, the official quarter, the residences of the native *daimyō*, its wide streets, and beautiful bay will always be looked upon with a certain degree of interest. Then, the views from the hills in its neighborhood are such as may well challenge comparison with those of any other town in Europe or elsewhere. Its suburbs, too, as I have already shown, are remarkable in many ways. Those beautiful valleys, wooded hills, and quiet lanes fringed with noble trees and evergreen hedges, would be difficult to match in any other part of the world.

Around Kanagawa

In due time I arrived at my old quarters in Kanagawa, and the plants I had purchased in Edo were delivered in good condition, and added to my other collections. Tunga and myself, with some Japanese whom I had taken into my service, were now daily ransacking the country in all directions in search of new plants and other ohiects of natural history.

One day, as I was returning from my rambles, the last part of my journey was along the Tōkaidō, which forms the main street of Kanagawa. In a teahouse on the roadside, a most curious operation was being performed, which attracted my attention. A woman was sitting with her back quite naked, while another of her sex was engaged in burning little puffs of a pithy-like combustible substance in four holes that had been made in the skin between the shoulders. To an European the operation would have been a most painful one; but the woman who was undergoing the treatment was laughing and joking as if she enjoyed it rather than otherwise. This was the moxa-burning treatment, frequently noticed in the works of Kaempfer and other writers on Japan. Moxa is said, in some books, to be made from the balls of a fungus, and in others to be furnished by the young leaves of wormwood (*Artemesia*). When used, it is in the form of little cones, which are placed in the holes above mentioned, and set on fire on the top. It bums slowly down, and leaves a blister on the skin, which afterwards breaks and discharges. The operation is considered very efficacious in preventing or curing the fevers of the country, as also in cases of rheumatism, gout, and even toothache. The Chinese irritate the skin for the same disorders by dipping the knuckles in hot tea, and pinching the neck, back, and other parts of the body until the skin becomes painfully tender.

Acupuncture is another famous remedy with the Japanese, although perhaps not so common or such an apparent luxury as the moxa-burning. It is used in cases of bowel complaint or colic, endemic to the country. This disease is supposed by them to be caused by wind, and, in order to let it out, several holes are made with needles in the muscles of the stomach or abdomen, and in other fleshy parts of the body. These needles are exceedingly fine, nearly as thin as hairs, and are generally made of gold or silver, although sometimes of steel by persons who profess to peculiar skill in tempering them. While the needles are passed through the skin and muscle, the nerves and blood-vessels are carefully avoided: a fact that shows the Japanese practitioners must have some knowledge of anatomy.

It is not unlikely that these two remedies for the common diseases of the country may, in many instances, prove useful; but I have no doubt the time is at hand when the Japanese will be taught to accomplish the objects they have in view in a way much more simple, and probably more efficiently. The medical men of Japan have always been remarkable for two things, when compared with the same class in China—they have always appreciated the higher character of the medical and surgical science of the Western nations, and have been attentive and eager students whenever they have had an opportunity of acquiring knowledge. Kaempfer, Thunberg, and Siebold all bear witness to this fact, and we have seen it further confirmed by the medical members of the Embassy who lately visited England, and who appear, by their visits to our hospitals and colleges, to have been most eager to acquire this kind of information. The only drawback to their obtaining a knowledge of surgery is their superstitious ideas; believing, as they do, that they become polluted by contact with dead bodies—a cir- cumstance that renders dissection impossible. Could this be got over, as it no doubt will be, their progress in the knowledge of surgery will be remarkable.

There are little roadside altars in many of the fields near Kanagawa, on which the natives burn incense, and offer salt, cash, and other things to a little deity rudely carved in stone. On one occasion I came up with three women, rather respectably dressed, and looking as if they belonged to the higher classes of Japan. They were accompanied by a man-servant, who carried in his hands a bundle of joss-sticks and paper as an offering to the god. They looked pleased to see a foreigner, were very polite, and asked me where I was going to, whence I came, and to what nation I belonged. On my returning the compliment by asking them the same questions, they informed me they had come from Kanagawa, and were about to offer incense at a little altar situated in a field some hundred yards ahead of us. Being anxious to witness the ceremony, I walked with them to the altar. When we reached the little stone god, one of the ladies, apparently the highest in rank, took the incense out of the hand of the servant, lighted it, and placed it in a stone basin in front of the image. She then bent low before the altar, all the time rubbing a string of beads she held in her hands and muttering some prayers. The second in rank stood behind her in a devout attitude, while behind the second stood the third, who made short work with her devotions, and laughed and talked to me while the others were engaged with their prayers. At the conclusion of the ceremony, which lasted only about two minutes, the three ladies pulled short tobacco-pipes out of their pockets, filled them with tobacco from their pouches, and begged me to give them a light from my cigar. I willingly complied with the request and, after having a comfortable little smoke together, we parted the best of friends.

It was now the end of May, and a considerable change had taken place in the appearance of the country. In the fields the barley was yellow, and ready for the sickle of the farmer in a few days; the rape-seed was ripe already and its harvest had commenced. The natives were busily employed in sowing and planting the summer crops between the rows of the standing com. These consist of soy and other beans, eggplants, sweet potatoes, cotton, melons and cucumbers, turnips, hill-rice, and sesame (*Sesamum orientale*).

The spring flowers had now all disappeared. The gorgeous peach and plum trees, whose falling petals strewed our path with flowers, were covered only with leaves; azaleas, camellias, violets, and primroses, and even the glorious glycine itself, had all passed by, and would not be seen again until the opening of another year. But although the spring beauties had gone by, another race, equally beautiful in its way, had come to take their places, to paint the woods and hedgerows and gardens with masses of gay colors, and to perfume the air with the fragrance of its blossoms. Wild roses were now in full flower. The hedges, banks, and uncultivated land were covered with their white blooms. A new species of weigela was growing wild everywhere, and was also in flower. In the end of May and in June *Deutzia scabra* and *Styrax japonica* are very beautiful. They abound on every hillside, in the hedges, and on the banks of streams. Later in the year the Styrax produces galls, from which a reddish dye is prepared. Honeysuckles, too (*Caprifolium japonicmn*) are abundant, and their flowers, with those of the wild rose, fill the air with delicious perfume.

In gardens, herbaceous peonies were out; several beautiful kinds of pinks, quite different from the spring sorts, were also in bloom, and there was a race of summer chrysanthemums which came in at this time, and which rendered the gardens extremely gay. In addition to these, I noted two fine new Weigelas, some clematises, irises. Spiraea Reeves tana, and the white Banksian rose. It is a common remark amongst foreigners that flowers are mostly scentless in Japan, and some have gone so far as to attribute this to the nature of the soil of the country. That this is not so will be apparent from the notices of the different fragrant plants abovementioned. Honeysuckles, roses (particularly the white Banksian), gardenias, peonies, tuberoses, and a hundred other flowers, are just as fragrant in Japan as they are elsewhere. Violets are scentless, but this appears to be the fault of the species, and not of the soil.

Before I left Edo a change seemed to be about to take place in the weather. Heavy clouds came up and hung over the city, and everyone acquainted with the climate of Japan predicted the near approach of the rainy season. The rains commenced on the night of the 26th of May, and continued to come down heavily during the whole of the following day. At 6 p.m. the clouds broke into masses, and the clear blue sky appeared above them.

That evening there appeared the most beautiful and perfect rainbow I had ever seen, and about the same time the clouds that rested on Mount Fuji gradually rose, and showed us the holy mountain basking in the evening sun, and still nearly covered with snow. One can scarcely imagine the beauty of the scene now spread out before me, and it was rendered more lovely and enjoyable by the fresh green foliage of the shrubs and trees, from whose leaves hung many thousands of pearly raindrops glistening in the sun's rays. Heavy rains were now of frequent occurrence, and continued at intervals up to the 15th of June. The rainy season seemed much more decided in its character here than in China; indeed it reminded me somewhat of the same season in India, although it did not last so long.

On the 1st of June I was awoke about three o'clock in the morning by an earthquake of a very violent character. Some rings suspended from a canopy in the temple first indicated the motion and began to tingle, then the whole building creaked and groaned, and lastly the bed on which I lay moved under me. It occurred at about three o'clock in the morning, and lasted for a few seconds only. Several other shocks were experienced afterwards during the morning, but these were much less violent, and some of them scarcely perceptible.

June 2nd.—The natives were still busy all over the fields, sowing and planting the summer crops between the rows of the ripening com. Blazing fires and dense clouds of smoke were now seen all over the country. The rape harvest was finished, the seed has been trampled out, and the farmers were now engaged in burning the stalks for the sake of the ashes, which are used as manure for the summer crops.

A nursery gardener who brought me a collection of plants that day for sale, had amongst them a genuine English strawberry covered with ripe fruit I have already had occasion to notice in an earlier chapter several foreign plants introduced from Western countries to Japan, as a proof of the enterprise of the people, but I was not aware until now that the real English strawberry was also here. A species of Fragaria is common, in a wild state, on the banks and hillsides, both in Japan and in China; but it has nothing to do with the species we cultivate in Europe, and is perfectly tasteless. Here, however, was the real simon-pure; and as many of the foreign residents had gardens round their houses, this discovery would enable them to have their strawberry beds, and to enjoy the old home luxury of strawberries and cream. I gladly purchased the plant in question, and carried it in triumph to the house of my friend Ross, with whom I was to dine.

How we placed it in the centre of the table, how we admired it, and what old scenes and old memories it brought before us, may be imagined by those who have been long resident in such far-off lands as Zipangu or Cathay.

During the remainder of the month of June I discovered and added to my collections several new plants of considerable interest, which I must now notice. One day I was out in the country in search of the seeds of a columbine, which were then ripe. In the grounds of a pretty little temple I came quite unexpectedly upon a new species of Deutzia having double rose-colored flowers. It was in full bloom at the time, and was very beautiful. The good priestess of the temple kindly allowed me to gather a few specimens of the flowers for my herbarium, and for a few *tempo* I induced her to part with some of the plants. This shrub will be hardy in England, and its double rose or pink colored blossoms will render it very ornamental in our gardens. Curiously enough I found at this time the pretty *Spircea callosa*, a shrub I had first seen on the Bohea Mountains in China, and which I had imported into Europe. It grows wild on the hillsides in Japan, and is also cultivated in gardens and much esteemed by the Japanese. Another *Spircea*—a herbaceous kind, resembling our own Queen of the Meadow, but with deep-red flowers—we also saw at this time. *Lychnis senno*, a plant I had known from a figure in Siebold's *Flora Japonica*, was also found in bloom, and added to my collections. It is cultivated in every cottage-garden, and is very showy and handsome when in bloom. Its leaves have a kind of violet hue somewhat resembling a Tradescantia, while its flowers are of a bright fiery red color. There are three varieties of this—a red, a white, and one with striped flowers. They are all very ornamental, particularly the striped one. I also saw Hydrangias, and a beautiful new honeysuckle, since named *Lonicera japonica*. Summer chrysanthemums were now hawked about the streets in great variety, many of them with large flowers, and some belonging to the class called Pompones. Irises were carried about in the same way; the natives being very fond of these, and having a number of fine kinds.

In the markets of Kanagawa and Yokohama there were now some good cucumbers and brinjals; two or three kinds of peas were in season, also French beans of first-rate quality. The summer fruits of Japan are few in number and inferior in kind. At this time we had wild raspberries and loquats (*Eriobotria japonica*). A little later two kinds of plums come in, some poor peaches, apricots, and melons. As a general rule all the summer fruits of Japan are very inferior to those in cultivation in England; but as, by the late treaty, we are now enabled to give the Japanese a sample of our manufactures, the time will, no doubt, come when we shall also improve their fruits and vegetables.

From the beginning to the end of June was the most successful time for our entomological collections. The moist air and warm sun brought out insects innumerable, and some of the common kinds of beetles might be shaken off the flowers or leaves of the trees by the thousand. Tunga and myself, assisted by troops of natives, were daily adding to our stores, and many cases were now crammed full of rare species, destined to instruct and, I hope, to give pleasure to many a western entomologist. I am indebted to Stevens, of Bloomsbury Street, London, for the names of a few of the more interesting species, in the following letter:

> The best insects you have brought from Japan comprise *Damaster* (new species), described by Adams as *D. Fortunei*, three species of true *Carabi* apparently undescribed, a new genus of the carabideous group allied to Sphodrus or Nebriay, two new species of Lucani or stag beetles, several new and beautiful Longicoms, a Spondylus allied to a species found in France and Germany, and interesting on that account; also several other coleoptera much resembling species found in England, and two or three species identical to English ones. Besides there is a most beautiful and apparently new butterfly, a species of Apaiura or an allied genus, of which the beautiful *A. Iris* (Purple Emperor) is found in England; some other butterflies almost identical with our own; and others resembling those found in the north and south of China. Many of the insects have a great resemblance to those found in China, and some are identical, including *Dynastes dichotoma*.

One afternoon about this time I came upon a group of countrymen, sitting under the shade of some trees, busily engaged in taking a kind of silk or gut from a large species of caterpillar. The animal was fully four inches long, its upper side was of a lively green color, while the under was white and covered with long white hairs. It feeds upon the leaves of a species of chesnut (*Castanea japonica*) very common on all the hillsides in this part of Japan. In the baskets containing the worms were a quantity of these leaves, which, judging from the rapid manner in which they were being eaten up, must be very palatable. But the curious part of the business remains to be told. These worms are not allowed to come to maturity, and then spin cocoons like the common silkworm, but each individual is disembowelled alive, and two short thread-like substances are taken out of its body. These threads are at first about three inches in length, and are covered thickly with a glutinous fatty substance. When dipped in a solution of some kind— apparently vinegar—this fatty matter comes readily off, and the threads are drawn out to their full length. Those which I measured on the spot were fully five feet long. I believe they are largely used in the manufacture of fishing lines, for which there is a considerable demand in Japan. The countrymen engaged in collecting them informed me they were also woven into articles of clothing, but if such be the case, which I think doubtful, such cloth must be very expensive.

The land-shells of Japan are of some interest to the conchologist, but the species are few in number, and not remarkable for their beauty. Cuming informs me that a Helix with a reversed mouth, which I have brought home, is *H. qucesito* (Deshayes), another is *Helix japonica* (Pfieffer), and a third, of which there are three varieties, is a new species, and undescribed. It is rather remarkable that a country like Japan, which abounds in woods, gardens, and waste lands, should have so few land-shells; such, however, is the case, as, had they been more plentiful, I think Tunga and myself must have met with them on our rambles.

During the last days of June and the first of July a small temple, adjoining that in which I was located, was daily crowded with natives who came to worship at its altars. The wheat and barley had been gathered in, the rice was planted, and I suppose the object of the festival was to praise Buddha for an abundant harvest, and to petition for a continuance of fine weather for the young paddy. Be this as it may, the people assembled in considerable numbers, for several days in succession, to take part in the worship. Here, as in other countries, the female portion of the community seemed to be the most numerous and the most devout, for certainly nine-tenths of this congregation were women. Many had their teeth blackened and their eyebrows pulled out, showing they were married, while others were still rejoicing in white teeth and single blessedness. Jolly-looking farmers' wives with their ruddy-cheeked daughters were there, mingling with the courtesans of the teahouses in gay dresses and painted faces. In China the priests perform the public services in the Buddhist temples and, if any of the people should chance to be present, they are there as spectators only. Here, the case was entirely different. Each worshipper was furnished with a cushion or hassock on which to kneel during his or, I should rather say, her devotions. A bit of round sounding brass was laid upon the cushion, and was struck by the devotee at certain times as the service went on. The priests led off, and then the whole congregation joined, striking their brass cymbals, and singing "*Nam, nam, nam,*" and some such unmeaning sounds, with their voices—unmeaning to me at least, for I did not understand them. The service lasted, each day, for about an hour, including an interval when the worshippers refreshed themselves with sundry copious draughts of *sake*.

On the 2nd of July, having heard the tinkling and "*nam, nam, nam*" going on for some time, I walked into the court in front of the little temple, in order to see something of the ceremonies. After remaining a few minutes I returned to my own quarters, and was soon followed by the whole con- gregation, who came, I suppose, to return my visit. Some amongst them were old men who could scarcely walk, but the greater part were women and children. I received them politely, and allowed them to examine my clothes, books, and specimens of natural history. One lady took hold of my wristband, another handled the neck of my shirt, and a third examined the texture of my trousers. But the butterflies, beetles, and shells were to them most astonishing and incomprehensible. Where could I have found such a number of these things?—many of which they had never seen before. What was I going to do with them? Was I going to eat them? Those who were wiser than the rest informed the others that I was collecting these things to make medicine! And then some stated that I had been over all the country gathering these objects; that I had been paying money for them—a statement that made some of them shake their wise heads, and evidently conclude that something was wrong with my "upper story." As all this was going on, the usual questions were put concerning my country, my age, and whether I was single or married. Many a goodhumored joke was, no doubt, passed round amongst them at my expense; but as my knowledge of the language was very limited, it amused them without doing me any harm. Then the good ladies wanted my opinion regarding themselves, and one after another was laughingly brought forward—married and single without distinction— and proposed as a helpmate. I took all this in good part, and eventually my visitors were reminded it was time to go back to their devotions. Then came a long series of "*He-hes*" and polite bowings, with many expressions of thanks, and I was left alone in my temple.

After leaving me, the congregation returned to the little temple in which they had been worshipping; and the singing, with the tinkling of bells and cymbals, went on as before. All at once the sounds ceased, and I concluded the services of the day were over. In this I was mistaken; for shortly afterwards I heard sounds of merriment, very different from those devotional ones that had preceded them. I was therefore induced to visit the congregation a second time, in order to satisfy my curiosity. When I reached the court in front of the temple a curious scene presented itself to my eyes. There was the same congregation in the same room in which they had been so devout a short time before, now engaged drinking *sake*, and already— judging from the loud laughter and the boisterous merriment—somewhat under its influence. When I was perceived in front of the door the intelligence was quickly passed round the room, and I was received by the assembly with a scream of delight. The hospitality of these people, in so far as *sake* was concerned, was boundless; and many invitations were given me to join the various groups, and to pledge them in cups of the favorite national stimulant. As *sake* is not a favorite of mine, I respectfully refused their offers with many thanks, and considered that the most prudent course for me to pursue, under the circumstances, would be to beat a retreat. But if I had any fears that this little carousal would end unpleasantly, these fears were perfectly groundless. At an appointed time the priests appeared in their robes of office, the *sake* that remained unconsumed was put away, the countenancers of the congregation changed from gay to grave—some of them, it is true, were a little more ruddy than before—and the religious services again commenced. The officiating priest led off, and was followed by his little congregation; and the *Nam-nam-nam*-ing, and tinkling of bells and cymbals, were kept up for about another hour. At the end of this time the people left the temple, and returned quietly to their homes.

Kamakura

A few miles south from Yokohama there is a pretty town named Kanazawa, and a little farther on is Kamakura, said to he the ancient capital of Japan. I had frequently heard of the beauty of these places, and more particularly of the scenery by which they were surrounded; and I therefore decided to visit them, and set out for this purpose on the 4th of July. On this occasion I was accompanied by Dr. Dickson from China, and Messrs. Ross and Hope, merchants in Yokohama. The first part of our road led us up through a beautiful valley, with richly-wooded hills dipping into it on either side, and giving it a pleasing and irregular outline. On the edges of this valley there were many cottages and farmhouses, and now and then we passed pretty glens that led up amongst the background of hills. Our road gradually ascended to a higher elevation; and when the highest point on the top of the hills was gained, we obtained a glorious view of scenery that reminded me of some of the prettiest spots in the Himalayas. We then continued our way along the ridge of the mountains, and looked down to the right and left upon valleys, glens, and round hills, all covered with the most luxuriant vegetation. I found a very beautiful new lily (*Lilium auratum*) on the hillsides in full bloom, and I dug up its roots and added it to my collections. Far away to the eastward the sea lay spread out before us, studded with islands, and dotted here and there with the white sails of junks and fishing boats. After we had travelled along the mountain ridge for some distance, the road began gradually to lead down hill, and about six o'clock in the evening we reached the village of Enazawa, which lies close upon the seashore.

Having engaged rooms at one of the principal inns of the place, we strolled out to look at the town. Kanazawa is a small place with a single street about half a mile in length, in which there are several inns and teahouses. This spot is remarkable and celebrated amongst the Japanese for its fine scenery. The sea comes in towards it between some small islands, and presents the appearance of a landlocked lake. Little hills, crowned with temples and trees, are studded about, from which charming views of sea and land scenery can be obtained. We ascended one of these, and were kindly received by the priests attached to the temple. Some fine fresh fruit of the loquat, and sundry cups of very good tea, were presented to us, and a visitors' book was brought in which to insert our names. This book contained the names of many distinguished Japanese who had honored the place with a visit; and numerous sketches and scraps of poetry, composed upon the spot, recorded the beauties of the situation and the fine views it commanded. The book was examined with much interest by the members of our little party, and Dr. Dickson proposed to buy it, offering the munificent sum of fourpence halfpenny as an inducement to the priest to part with it. The Japanese are certainly a curious people; they will sell anything for money. The priest took the tempos and Dickson carried off the visitors' book with its valuable autographs, clever sketches, and immortal poetry. After visiting some other places of interest, we returned to our inn, having been everywhere received with the greatest politeness by the people.

We occupied a suite of rooms upstairs. They communicated with each other by sliding doors made of paper pasted over a wooden frame; these doors could be taken out, and the whole flat converted into one room when required. The room in which we dined looked out upon the sea, and the high road of the town was under our windows. As the weather was exceedingly warm, the windows were out, and we were fully exposed to the sea-breeze and to a crowd of natives of both sexes and of all ages who crowded the road in front of the inn. After dinner we sat on a ledge at the window, and amused ourselves with the crowd below. Strange questions were put to us on many subjects; and as the Japanese, as a people, have not our ideas of morality, many of their questions and remarks were not such as I can repeat here. Our landlord, who was probably better acquainted with our manners and customs than the crowd under his windows, several times expostulated with them in an angry tone, but produced no effect. Once or twice a bucket of water was added to his arguments; but although this induced them to scamper away for an instant, they soon came back again. As the night wore on the crowd gradually dispersed, and, intending to be up early next morning, we followed their example and retired to rest.

The floors of our bedrooms were covered with clean matting, and a padded counterpane was laid in the middle of each room, with a wooden pillow for the head to rest upon. Ample mosquito curtains, nearly as large as the room itself, reached from the ceiling to the floor.

Next morning at daylight we were up, and in order to refresh ourselves, we had a plunge in the bay. As we intended to proceed intimidately after breakfast across the hills to the ancient town of Kamakura, I employed the time before our meal was ready in visiting several places of interest in the vicinity in search of new plants. In the grounds of a native lord here I observed some trees of *Podocarpus macrophyllus* of great size, some fine examples of *Pirms massoniana*, and a new Arborvitae (*Thuja falcata*).

The town of Kamakura was distant from Kanazawa some five miles. We sent our horses onward by the lower route, and chose the hill road ourselves, in order to get a better view of the surrounding country. After leaving the valley this road led us gradually upwards, and then along a ridge of hills somewhat like those we had noticed the day before on the journey from Yokohama. When we had attained a considerable elevation, the views on all sides were exceedingly fine and extensive. On our right hand and on our left we looked down upon and over a perfect sea of hills, of all sizes and of every conceivable form, covered, from their summits to the valleys below, with trees and brushwood. Many of these forests had been planted and were now yielding valuable timber, but by far the greatest portion of them were in a state of nature, very beautiful to look upon no doubt, but covered with wild trees and dense brushwood of little value. Far away down in the valleys we observed patches of cultivated land, which, taken in connection with our mountain road and the forests that had been planted, were the only marks of the country being inhabited by man. We did not meet one single human being during this part of our journey.

The climate is one of the finest in the world; and the soil fertile and capable of growing excellent timber, and of yielding abundant crops of grain. How can this state of things be accounted for, if we believe the statements of Thunberg, Kaempfer, Siebold, and other travellers, that the country is densely populated? But the travellers with the Dutch embassies from Nagasaki to Edo rarely left the imperial highway on their route, and must have received their impressions from what they observed as they went along it, and from the crowded state of the great towns through which they passed. Anyone, even now, whose experience of Japan was confined to the Tōkaidō, would come to the same conclusion; but let them leave the great highway and penetrate into the country by its common roads, and then some doubts would probably come across their mind on the subject. And if they happen to know anything about agriculture or woodlands, and sees, on every hand, thousands of goodly acres, capable of producing crops of corn or valuable timber, lying waste or only covered with brushwood of little value, they will at least affirm that there are in that country the means of supplying all the necessaries of life to a population far greater than that which exists in Japan at the present day.

When we reached the highest land on our journey, we left the road and mounted the top of an adjoining hill, from which may be obtained one of the finest views in Japan. On the south was the sea, with the beautiful little island of Enoshima, famous in Japanese history; to the west was a chain of mountains, with Fuji-*yama* towering high above them all; while, far away in the east, the capital itself may be seen on a clear day. Down in the valley below us we could discern the roofs of the houses and temples of Kamakura, the ancient capital of the country, to which we were bound.

Having rested for a while on this beautiful spot, and enjoyed the view spread out before us, we set out again on our journey. The road now led down the mountainside, a portion of the way in a ravine, down which a clear stream was running, shaded with lofty trees. At length we reached Kamakura, which presents, at the present day, no appearance of having once been a capital town. It is simply a country village, with a few mean shops and some good inns or teahouses. But its temples and the scenery in the neighborhood will always render it a place of great attraction to foreign visitors, as it has been for ages to the Japanese. It is situated at the head of a valley, with hills on each side and behind, and open in front to the sea. A fine avenue of pine trees extends from the temples down to the beach.

Handsome broad roads intersect each other and this avenue at right angles, and these are also fringed on each side with clumps and rows of trees. *Cryptomeria japonica*, *Pinus massonia*, and *Salisburia adiantifolia* are the trees generally used for these avenues.

As we entered the village a most extraordinary circumstance occurred, which took us entirely by surprise, until we remembered that we were in Japan. A woman rushed out of a shop and placed herself in the middle of the road, holding a tobacco pipe in one hand, and a box containing some tobacco and sundry other articles in the other. When I first saw her my impression was, that she either meant to welcome us by the offer of her pipe, or that she wished to dispose of the wares in her box. But such was not her intention. To our alarm and surprise, she threw off the only garment she wore and assumed the attitude of a naked statue, at the same time putting her pipe into her mouth and puffing out clouds of tobacco smoke. The people came running towards us from every part of the village, and were evidently accustomed to such exhibitions on the part of the individual before us. When we recovered from our surprise we came to the conclusion that the poor creature was insane, which we afterwards found to be the case.

As the day was cloudless, with the thermometer standing somewhere about 100° in the shade, we were glad to take up our quarters in a teahouse. We were welcomed by the host and some pretty maidens, and conducted up stairs to a suite of rooms with open windows looking out upon the village. While we were sitting fanning ourselves and enjoying the shade, after the fierce heat to which we had been exposed for some hours, crowds of people assembled on the road in front of the inn, all anxious to get a glimpse of their foreign visitors. All at once there seemed some commotion amongst them, and they rushed away to look at someone who was coming towards our inn by a cross road not visible from the rooms we occupied. At first we thought this excitement was caused by a fresh arrival of foreigners from Kanagawa, who had promised to come after us and join our party. Presently, however, our mad friend came in sight, carrying in her arms a bundle of branches and some sticks of incense, as if she contemplated paying a visit to the temples or to the tombs. Poor thing! she seemed to be good-humored and harmless in her insanity; and even the little children, although they ran away when she approached them, did not seem much afraid of her. She soon returned from the temples, and then employed herself in fetching water and pulling grass and weeds for our horses, which were tied up on the roadside in front of the inn. While engaged in this operation she seemed to fancy that the horses were fit objects of adoration; and as she fed each animal with grass, or gave it water, she closed her hands in an attitude of devotion, and muttered to it some Buddhist form of prayer.

When we had rested a short time in the inn we rode out to pay a visit to the Kamakura Daibutsu, a large bronze statue considered one of the lions of the district. We found this situated in a pretty garden about two miles from Kamakura. When we reached the entrance to the grounds we were politely requested to dismount, as no one was allowed to ride into the sacred enclosure. We entered the garden and proceeded up a paved walk lined on each side with fine specimens of trees and shrubs, many of which were trained and clipped into curious forms. At the head of the garden stood, or rather sat, the enormous bronze image we were seeking. It was not less than thirty feet in diameter at the base, and fully forty feet in height. The proportions of the figure were admirable. At first sight we were astonished at the size of the casting, but upon a closer examination we found that the huge colossus had been cast in several parts, and then joined together or built up.

An old priest who lived in a small temple adjoining told us that this figure had been placed there six hundred years ago; and no doubt, had we been better acquainted with the language of the country, we might have learned some curious particulars of its history. A door at one of the sides led into the interior. This was opened by the priest, and we were invited to enter along with him. We found the inside lighted by windows placed at the back; and there were many ornaments—such as small gilded images representing Buddhist deities, and strips of paper—hanging on the walls. Boxes were placed here for the offerings of the devotees who visit the shrine. Indeed these are found in nearly all the temples of Japan, just as they are met with in the churches of Christian countries. Altogether, the place, the scenery, and the statue, well rewarded us for our visit; and our only regret on coming away was that we could learn so little of the origin and history of this remarkable place.

This part of the country abounds in temples, and in that respect was more fitted for the site of the capital of the emperor than for that of a *shōgun*. We visited another temple in the course of the morning, not far from the bronze statue, and were shown some large tinselly-looking images that were evidently thought wonderful things by the country people. One of the most remarkable was kept in a dark place, which had to be lighted up when it was visited—another mode of getting contributions from the devout. Lithographs of this goddess were also on sale in the temple.

In Japan, as in China, noisy crowds followed us into the sacred buildings, and were anything but reverential in their demeanor. With all their noise they were good-homored enough, and not at all unfriendly in their manner towards us. Other temples were pointed out in various directions, which we were pressed to visit; but as the day was oppressively hot, and as we had the dread of fever before our eyes, we rode back to our inn at Kamakura, determined to keep indoors until the sun's rays were less powerful.

We had ordered luncheon before we set out, and on our return we found a most substantial meal awaiting us. It consisted of excellent fish fresh from the sea, cooked in the soy of the country, and most delicious it was; fine white rice; and an omelette, rather too sweet perhaps, but very palatable. This we washed down with delicious cold water from the well of the inn, mixed with a little brandy which we had brought with us, and which we preferred to the *sake* of the country. No knives or forks, or rude things of that kind, seen at the tables of Western barbarians, were known at our inn at Kamakura. Chopsticks, those useful and civilized implements which feed more than four hundred millions of the human race, were the only articles used during our repast. More than one of my companions complained of the awkwardness of these instruments; but as I had been accustomed to their use in China, I took kindly to them in Japan. During the time of our meal we were waited upon by the ladies of the inn. Truth compels me to state that they were not particularly handsome, but nevertheless they were most kind and obliging, and very active in anticipating all our wants.

Fatigued with the exertions of the morning, we laid ourselves down on the clean white mats covering the floors of our apartments, and were soon in the enjoyment of a comfortable siesta. I was the first to awake, and on looking into the room adjoining mine a curious and amusing scene presented itself. One of my companions was lying sound asleep, while the poor maniac whose acquaintance we had made in the morning was kneeling by his side, fanning his head, and every now and then pausing in this operation to clasp her hands together and mutter some words of prayer, either to him or for him, as she had done to the horses in the morning. The most amusing part of the performance was to see our friend lying perfectly unconscious of the honors that were being paid to him. The poor woman had also brought up four cups of tea and a handful of dry rice, which she laid upon the ground as an offering to our party. As soon as she saw us awake and noticing her movements, she rose quietly and walked out of the room without paying the slightest attention to any of us.

When the day had become a little cooler we left the shelter of our inn and went to pay a visit to the temples for which Kamakura is celebrated all over the empire of Japan. They are placed at the head of the valley before-mentioned, and are approached by an avenue terminating in a broad flight of stone steps in front of the temples. They are eight in number, and are only opened, we were told, once or twice a year. We did not observe any priests about them, nor any signs of Buddhist worship; and therefore they probably belonged to the Shintō sect, the ancient religion of Japan. Their roofs are remarkable in form, and one of them has a tower somewhat like an Indian minaret. Although we could not enter these temples, we could look through the bars of their doors and see their contents. Many of them contained wooden images of different kinds, some of which were supposed to cure certain diseases, and were worshipped and prayed to by the afflicted. One in particular was pointed out which could cure ophthalmia, and we were gravely assured by our guide that anyone afflicted with sore eyes, which are very common in Japan, as well as in China, had only to look upon this image and be healed.

Among the other wonders of the place was a sacred stone, curiously formed by nature, and apparently slightly assisted by art. This stone had the remarkable property, we were told, of rendering barren women fruitful. Ladies came from afar to worship it, and at the same time to turn their faces towards the holy mountain, which is said to be one of the conditions to ensure a successful issue. A box is duly provided for the reception of offerings, which shows that there is someone who is prepared to profit by the superstitions of his countrywomen. We are surprised and we pity the poor Japanese for their superstitious delusions, and yet, if one of them were to write an account of his travels amongst ourselves, could he not tell his countrymen that in enlightened England, in the nineteenth century, a class of persons gain a livelihood by telling the fortunes of our servant girls, and sometimes of their mistresses, and promising them rich husbands, horses and carriages, and lots of romping children? With these things in our minds we should not be too hard on the superstitions of the good ladies who visit the sacred stone at Kamakura.

The afternoon was now getting cool, for the sun was sinking rapidly behind the western hills. We therefore returned to our inn, paid our bill, mounted our horses, and took the lower road for Kanazawa, the place where we had lodged the night before. As we were leaving Kamakura I rode up to the foot of a hill on our left to see the tomb of Minamoto no Yoritomo, a celebrated general, the founder of the race of *shōguns*, and a man who is remembered among the people as William Wallace or Robert Bruce is in Scotland.

Yoritomo's tomb is placed near the base of a hill in a charming situation. Behind it and on each side were trees and brushwood, while in front were green ricefields extending down to the seashore, the little town of Kamakura with its temples and avenues lying between. It was approached by a flight of steps, and consisted of a small plain stone tower surrounded by a dwarf wall. The whole edifice was hoary with age, having probably been erected upwards of six hundred years ago. And this was the resting-place of a general of great renown, the first of the race of *shōguns*, and a man whose memory is still cherished by the natives of Japan.

Our lowland road back to Kanazawa was a very pleasant one, leading us at one time along the banks of a clear stream, and at another through some natural gap or deep cutting in the hills. We spent a second night in our inn, and on the following day returned to Kanagawa.

Richardson's Murder

On our arrival at Kanagawa we were startled by the intelligence that the British legation at Edo had been attacked the night before by a band of *rōnin*, and that the lives of Her Majesty's minister and his staff of assistants had been in the greatest danger. From the assassinations which had taken place on several occasions, both at Edo and at Yokohama, since these places had become the residences of foreigners, human life was generally regarded as being somewhat insecure. And what made matters worse was the fact that no one could give any satisfactory reason for these murders. True, it was reported that Alcock's servant, who was one of the first victims, had given offense by his arrogance and overbearing manner; the murder of two Russians was attributed to a Japanese official, who, with his family, was degraded at the instance of Count Muravyov, in consequence of some insult offered to the Russians in the streets of Edo; and the assassination of the American secretary of the legation was said to have been committed by a *daimyō*'s retainer, struck by him in the street, who, on returning to his master, was asked how he dared to do so after receiving a blow that was still unavenged. Offense may have been given in this way, and the Japanese, who are a proud and revengeful people, would most certainly have their revenge. But none of the foreign residents could actually affirm that insults of this kind were the causes of the melancholy events that followed.

Taking for granted that those who had fallen victims to revenge had done something to merit their punishment, it does not follow that the innocent in Japan may always consider themselves perfectly safe. The Japanese assassin is not particular as to his victim. If he can secure the real offender, good and well; if not, a substitute must be had; if an Englishman give offense and cannot be found, one of his countrymen must suffer in his stead. This being the state of affairs, it is plain that the innocent may, at any time, suffer for the imprudence or follies of his countrymen, or, indeed, of any foreigner, without respect to nationality; for the avenger is not particular even on that point.

Revenge is a powerful feeling in the breasts of the natives of Japan, more particularly amongst the higher classes and their numerous bands of two-sworded retainers. These gentry are always ready to resent an insult or injury, real or supposed; and as each man carries about his person two swords whose edges are extremely sharp, he has always the means of giving instant effect to his passion. Nor does this desire for revenge end with the life of the injured person. On the contrary, if he has not been able to accomplish it during his lifetime, he will leave it as an inheritance and obligation to his relations. In the autumn of 1860, Michael Moss, an English merchant, who was returning from a shooting excursion, was seized on his way by the native police, and charged with having broken the laws of the country, no one being allowed to shoot within a certain distance of Edo. In attempting to disarm him, a loaded gun went off, and lodged its contents in the arm of one of the officials. The wound was a dangerous one, and the foreign doctors of the place were of opinion that, unless amputation was resorted to, the man would, in all probability, lose his life. This advice, for some reason, was not listened to; but, luckily, owing to a good constitution, or perhaps to diet, the dreaded mortification did not take place, and the man recovered. It was stated to us at the time of this occurrence that the wounded man had taken an oath that, should he recover, he would not rest until he had the merchant's life, and that, should he die, his brothers would take care that he was avenged. The gentleman in question was tried at the British consulate and sentenced to deportation; and to this sentence he probably owed his life, which, after what had happened, was not safe for an hour in Japan. During my residence in Japan there were several other instances in which foreigners were obliged to take a hasty leave of the country in order to save their lives.

But although we knew the Japanese to be proud and revengeful, and not very particular as to the identity of their foes provided they were foreigners, and although the community had to deplore the murder of several of its members, apparently innocent and unoffending men, yet nothing had taken place recently to give us any uneasiness. The Japanese, we fancied, were getting accustomed or resigned to the presence of foreigners amongst them; or our rough manners—at times somewhat frolicsome and boisterous—were seen to be harmless, and not intended to hurt or annoy them. But when the news of the murderous attack on the British legation reached us, the scales fell at once from our eyes, and we saw we had been sitting in fancied security on the top of a mine which was liable to an explosion at any moment.

Various and contradictory accounts of the attack reached us at Kanagawa. As an authentic account has however been sent home by Alcock to Earl Russell and presented to both Houses of Parliament, I cannot do better than give an extract from it to the reader in Alcock's own words:

Edo, July 6, 1861.—Before another night closes in, with its contingencies, which may well prevent my addressing your Lordship again, I am anxious to submit a simple statement of the events which have marked the last; for, whether I survive or not, it is essential that Her Majesty's government should be well and duly informed of all that has taken place. We have escaped a massacre, but, seemingly, by the merest chance.

I had only returned from Kanagawa four-and-twenty hours, bringing George Morrison and another gentleman with me, on a visit to Edo—the legation being further augmented by Laurence Oliphant and Russell—when the long-threatened onslaught roused us all from our beds a little before midnight. Frequently as I had been warned that such a deed was actually in contemplation, I confess I felt incredulous when Robertson, who, previous to his retiring to rest, always takes the duty of going through the premises, came to tell me that there was a conflict going on outside, and that men were forcing their way through the gates. I had barely time to seize my revolver and advance a few steps, when I heard blows and cries, and the report of a pistol in the passage that runs at the end of my apartment. The next moment both Oliphant and Morrison staggered forward, exclaiming that they were wounded, and I saw the blood flowing profusely from the former, whose left arm was disabled.

Russell, Robertson, and Lowder followed; the rest of the legation were missing. Uncertain how many our assailants were, or from how many quarters the attack might be effected (since a Japanese house is open on all sides, and every partition consists entirely of doors and windows only, or sliding-panels offering no resistance), a brief interval of intense anxiety followed, while I stood in momentary expectation of seeing men pour in from the passage in pursuit. After a short lull, some of the band were heard outside the apartment adjoining my bedroom breaking their way through some glazed doors. Exposed to attack from every side, with no sign of a *yakunin* or guard, several minutes were thus passed, two of our number disabled, and the rest of us standing at bay with such arms as had been hastily seized. Our enemies had evidently mistaken their way, and the increased distance of the shouts and yells gave reason to hope they had at last been come up with by the *yakunin*, and had sought their safety by leaving the house. To escape from a state of intolerable suspense I went towards the principal entrance for a moment, and to Macdonald's room, to ascertain, if possible, what had become of him. While on my way we thought they had returned in force, seeing at the further end of the passage a number of armed men advancing, who would not answer our challenge. A shot was fired by Lewder, and they disappeared. Still the noise and clamor and conflict continued outside; and it seemed very long indeed before we saw any of those (to the number of some 150) *shōgun*'s and *daimyō*'s men who had been held to afford us such ample protection! At last, two or three of the officers permanently on service appeared to say that they hoped the house was clear, but begging us to keep together at one end while they made further search.

I had now a moment of respite to turn to Laurence Oliphant and George Morrison and dress their wounds, though amidst alarms of renewed attack, which, I may add, recurred at frequent intervals until daybreak. . . . Most providentially the party, which seems to have been destined to penetrate the interior of the house and finish the work there, mistook their way to the part occupied by myself from the beginning, and where all who remained after the first alarm were speedily collected, as the most defensible position. Had they entered the grounds from that side (and nothing was easier), steps and a path led directly to my bedroom, and I should have most likely had no time to seize a weapon, for there was nothing to obstruct their entrance.

Fortunately for the little band in the legation, the Japanese guard, when it arrived, fought bravely, and the assailants were driven out of the premises. It would seem, therefore, that, owing to this on the one hand, and to the ignorance of the locality on the part of the *rōnin* on the other, a general massacre was happily prevented.

> The next morning the legation looked as if it had been sacked after a serious conflict. Screens and mats were all spotted with blood, the former thrown down, broken, and torn; furniture and bedding all hacked, books even cut through by their sabres, and the marks of fury and violence everywhere. That our guards fought, there is no doubt whatever; but it is equally clear that they were, as I always asserted, utterly ineffective against a surprise; and, in truth, they left the legation, notwithstanding their great superiority in numbers, at least ten minutes to its own resources, during which time the *rōnin* were in possession trying to discover the inmates.

It does not appear that the loss of life was very great in this hand-to-hand encounter between the *yakunin* and *rōnin*, a circumstance that may possibly be accounted for by the attack taking place during the night of the *shōgun's* and *daimyō's* men, two were killed and ten wounded; three of the *rōnin* were nearly hacked to pieces, two wounded men were taken prisoners, and it was rumored that two more committed *harakiri* next morning to avoid being arrested. The whole band of the attacking *rōnin* was afterwards ascertained to have been fourteen in number.

Alcock writes:

> After such a night comes a governor of Foreign Affairs, deputed from the ministers, gravely to felicitate me on my escape and return to

Edo, praying me to accept a basket of ducks and a jar of sugar in token of amity! Your Lordship will, I am sure, not blame me, that I desired the messenger to take his presents back with him, and tell his principal I desired justice and redress, not ducks or sugar, at the hands of his government.

When the news of this attempted assassination reached us at Kanagawa and Yokohama, the sensation created, both amongst natives and foreigners, was very great. Who were the *rōnin*, and who or what had induced them to attempt the commission of such a fearful crime? Alcock and the Dutch Consul-General Jan Karel de Wit had just come overland from Osaka, although the government had begged them not to do so, and warned them of the danger of such a proceeding at the present time. Great offense had been given, it was said, by their visit to one of the *daimyō* of Mito's coalmines, although the road to it had been blocked up by a bamboo fence with a guard of soldiers behind it. It was also rumored that a dispute for precedence had occurred on the road with a *daimyō*, who happened to be met travelling in a contrary direction, although it now appears from Alcock's despatch that he had given way to the great man, and for his politeness had been almost pushed into the ditch! As these reports were spread about, it was the opinion of many that this overland journey, in some way or other, had been the cause of the attack that had just taken place. On the other hand, it was argued, and with some reason, that, had the government or offended *daimyō* been the authors or instigators of the crime, it might have been much more easily and effectually accomplished on the journey than in the British legation at Edo.

In connection with this question there was a document found on one of the *rōnin* who was wounded and made prisoner, to which a considerable amount of importance is due. Four translations of this document were made; one being official, while the other three were obtained from private sources. In the official copy the writer says:

He is a man of low degree, moved by the desire to do a great deed in honor of the sovereign—to expel the foreigner, as it is intolerable to stand by and see the sacred empire violated by the barbarians. To achieve honor for himself, as a devoted patriot, making the empire

to sparkle in foreign regions by a great deed, while tranquillizing the Imperial mind, and benefiting the country by ridding it of the presence of the foreigner.
—for these objects this worthy is willing to risk his life.

The translations furnished by private individuals are similar to the above; but one or two important things come out that would appear to have been suppressed in the official copy. Thus the writer does not say that he is "moved by the desire to do a great deed in honor of the sovereign," but "To follow out my master's will." In two of the private translations he takes it for granted that, if he can massacre the officers of the British legation, "all foreigners will abandon Japan," or "the land of the gods," and so procure him the favor of millions of his countrymen.

This paper appears to have been considered a genuine document by the Japanese authorities, and not, as some supposed, put into the man's pocket as a blind to mislead investigation as to the instigators of the deed. In one of their letters to Alcock they say:

Although your Excellency suggested that the attack was not made spontaneously on the part of the assailants, but that there was a secret director of it; yet, as we have always communicated to you, it was known that, in the early period of the opening of the ports, there were, among the persons of rank, some who disapproved of the conclusion of the treaties with foreign powers.

Then they go on to state that, owing to the arrangements made from time to time by the government, this prejudice amongst the higher ranks has entirely disappeared—an assertion which, I fear, is not founded on fact, and that:

the occurrence is only ascribable to the acts of persons of low standing, who, from obstinate adhesion to the old custom of excluding foreign powers, persist in their feelings of partiality. The alteration in their nature will therefore be difficult, without allowing a long lapse of months and years.

The Japanese ministers remind Alcock that they had proposed to him in the beginning, when officers for his protection were appointed, their wish that a guard should be stationed, not only in the environs of the legation, but even in the interior. "But your Excellency was altogether dissatisfied with it; so we left it to your will: hence the danger which has just happened." And thus these worthies prove three things, apparently to their own satisfaction:

1st, that persons of high rank were not the instigators of the deed; 2nd, that it was the work of prejudiced enthusiasts of low degree; 3rd, that, had the English minister taken their advice, the thing would not have happened.

Alcock, "after three weeks consumed in anxious inquiries as to the quarter from whence blow had come and any future danger might be looked for," believes he has at last got at the real facts. In a despatch to Earl Russell he says:

It has come to me from divers sources that the *daimyō* of Tsushima, hearing that a great chief of the foreigners was at Nagasaki on his way to Edo overland, immediately despatched emissaries to slay this chief on the road, and bring his head…But I think the more recent versions of the story are also the more probable. These tell me that the *daimyō* only sent a single emissary to follow me to Edo, and there to find the fit instruihents for his purpose (never far to seek, it seems), and bring him my head, after the massacre of everyone about me. A plot to attack the legations, the consulates, or Yokohama, together or successively, having long been a favourite plan among Mito's disbanded followers and other desperate characters, it required but a signal from any chief immediately to get together the men necessary for an attack; and so it was suddenly resolved upon and carried into execution at the instigation of the *daimyō* 's emissary.

The true version of this story, whatever it may be, will probably never be known to foreigners, but that this is something near it there can be little doubt. I firmly believe the real instigator of the crime was some feudal prince, who was still hostile to foreigners, or perhaps was not unwilling to embroil his own government in a quarrel which he supposed would in some way advance his interests. A feudal system exists in Japan at the present day not unlike that of our own Scottish Highlands a hundred years ago; and any chief can easily excite the passions of his retainers, and engage them in the most desperate enterprises.

In a country like Japan, where everyone acts as a spy upon his neighbour, it seems absurd to suppose that the government was unable to find out the instigator of the attack on the British legation. Whether it durst denounce and punish was a very different matter, and extremely doubtful. Instead of being at once united and powerful, as it was at one time supposed to be, it resembles that of the Scottish kings in the feudal ages, when a combination of the powerful clans could always embarrass or overturn the government. In addition to this, some of the *daimyō* would seem to derive their honors and offices directly from the emperor and to be, to a certain extent, independent of the *shōgun*. These, by way of fomenting troubles, ply the emperor's court with disturbing rumors to the disadvantage of the rival but confessedly subordinate court at Edo; and keep up the smouldering embers of a still possible explosion in the renewal of the old struggles between the true sovereign and the usurping general-in-chief, each backed by their partizans amongst the *daimyō*. This, therefore, is another element of weakness in the government of Japan. We may, therefore, easily suppose that the government well knew the instigator of the attack on the legation, and yet was afraid or unable to punish him.

With these difficulties to contend with, particularly in their relations with foreign powers and their subjects, the task of the ministers of the *shōgun* is not exactly an agreeable one. I believe they are sincere in their endeavours to protect foreigners from the dangers that surround them on every side, owing to the hatred and fanaticism of unfriendly *daimyō* and their retainers. Doubtless their suggestion to Alcock to have a guard inside the legation was well meant; and their plan of surrounding the new settlement of Yokohama, and placing guards on the different approaches—which some people found so much fault with—was intended for our protection. They knew the dangers to which we were exposed much better than we did ourselves, and took their own mode of averting them.

But in the present state of Japan, with the feudal system in full operation, with jealousies existing amongst the nobles, with bands of idle retainers roaming about the streets, always armed and not over-friendly to foreigners, the task of protecting us is no easy one. Those ministers who agreed to make treaties with foreign nations did not foresee the difficulties and dangers they had to encounter in opening up a country that had been sealed to the rest of the world for nearly three hundred years. The future is now enveloped in thick darkness, but it is much to be feared that war and all its horrors may, at no distant day, be the penalty this happy and peaceful land will have to paty for a reintroduction to the great family of nations.

While these pages have been going through the press the overland mail has brought us an account of another brutal murder, which was perpetrated on the Tōkaidō, within a few miles of Edo, on the 14th of September last. The murderers in this case were the retainers of of Shimazu Hisamitsu, the father of the *daimyō* of Satsuma, and he is stated personally to have given the atrocious order. The following narrative of this sad transaction is taken from the *Japan Herald*:

> Yesterday afternoon, about two o'clock, a party left Yokohama for a country ride, intending to cross to Kanagawa in a boat, and proceed thence on horseback to Kawasaki, where there is a fine temple. The party was composed of Mrs. Borradaile, the wife of a merchant at Hongkong; Marshall, her brother-in-law, a merchant of Yokohama; W. Clarke, of the house of Messrs. A. Heard and Co.; and Richardson, who had just retired from business in China, and was on a visit to Japan, prior to his return to England. The community, at about half-past three o'clock in the afternoon, were startled by the return of Mrs. Borradaile on horseback at Gower's house, in a fearful state of agitation and disorder, her hands, face, and clothes bespattered with blood, her hat gone, and in a fainting state. She informed Mr. Gower that she had just ridden for her life over seven miles, and had escaped she knew not how from a most dastardly and murderous attack upon herself and her companions; that about four miles beyond Kanagawa, nearly halfway to Kawasaki, they had met part of a *daimyō*'s train, consisting of a large body of two-sworded men, coming from Edo,

some of whom signed to them to move aside, which they did. They drew up their horses at the side of the road, but in consequence of continued signs to go back they turned their horses to return towards Kanagawa. Without a word, or the slightest further notice, some of the retainers drew their swords and fiercely attacked them. A cut was aimed at Mrs. Borradaile's head, which she fortunately avoided by quickly stooping, though her hat was cut away by the blow. The three gentlemen were badly wounded, and being entirely surrounded, and the road being for some distance lined by their assailants, and being themselves entirely unarmed, they had no course but to dash through them, and to endeavour thus to effect their escape. Mrs. Borradaile saw Richardson fall from his horse, as she supposed, dead, and the others were so badly wounded that Marshall told her to ride for her life and try to save herself, as he did not think they could keep up. She scarcely remembers what happened afterwards, but she recollects riding into the sea, preferring the risk of drowning to falling into the hands of these bloodthirsty miscreants. Her horse, however, regained the road, and continued his headlong course towards Yokohama, twice falling under her. By some means she regained her seat, and arrived, fainting and exhausted, at the house mentioned. Fortunately Dr. Jenkins and Gower's brother entered the house at the moment, the former of whom administered the needful restoratives; and Gower s brother, at her earnest entreaties, went at once to Captain Vyse to endeavour to obtain assistance towards the recovery of the persons of her companions, all those of whom he imagined were lying dead in the road. The report at once flew round the settlement; and having learnt from others coming from Kanagawa that two of the party were lying dangerously wounded at the American Consulate at that place, while the third had been left weltering in his blood on the road, some three miles beyond, a large body of residents of all nationalities collected, and immediately started by water and by land for Kanagawa. Among the first was Dr. Jenkins, of Her Majesty's legation, who had immediately procured his instruments to render what aid might lie in his power. On arriving at the American Consulate they found

Marshall severely wounded in the side and back, while Clarke's left arm at the shoulder was nearly cut through, the sword having penetrated half through the bone. Their wounds, however, had been immediately attended to and dressed by Dr Hepburn, of the American mission. From what was gathered from Clarke, the few who had arrived determined at once to proceed in search of Richardson, who had been seen by him also to fall from his horse exhausted. As they reached the main road they perceived Captain Vyse, accompanied by several residents on horseback, together with the mounted guard, proceeding on the same errand…They continued on the road till they arrived at the half-way house between Kanagawa and Kawasaki, where they were joined by the French mounted guard, who had received orders from M. de Bellecourt, His Imperial Majesty's Envoy, to act in concert with Captain Vyse and those who accompanied him. Here they made inquiries, but could get no information, the people afflicting entire ignorance upon the matter. A little boy, however, came forward and volunteered to point out where the body was lying; under his guidance they retraced their step, about half a mile and found the body lying about ten yards off the road in a field, at the side of a small cottage. It was covered over with a couple of old mats, which, on being removed, revealed a most ghastly and horrible spectacle. The whole body was one mass of blood; one wound, from which the bowels protruded, extended from the abdomen to the back; another, on the left shoulder, had severed all the bones into the chest; there was a gaping spear-wound over the region of the heart; the right wrist was completely divided, and the hand was hanging merely by a strip of flesh; the back of the left hand was nearly cut through; and on moving the head, the neck was found to be entirely cut through on the left side. 'The two first-mentioned wounds had evidently been the first he had received, and had been given while he was on horseback; the last four, or certainly two of them, had been inflicted after he had fallen from his horse, if not after death. A litter having been hastily constructed, the party returned to Kanagawa with the body.

Poor Richardson! I knew him well. He was a fine manly specimen of a young Englishman, of a mild and conciliatory disposition, and not at all likely to give any wanton offense to the Japanese people. Why then was the party attacked, and why this brutal murder? They were riding along the Tōkaidō, within the limits of the settlement provided by treaty with the government of the *shōgun*, and were apparently infringing no law. Perhaps their great offense was this: they did not turn back or out of the way quick enough when they saw the cortage of the great man approaching. But although this was probably the pretext for attacking them, other causes, lying far deeper than this, were not wanting. These are an intense hatred to foreigners of Western nations, and a dread of those innovations and changes that are seen to be coming upon the country, and that will eventually destroy the feudal power.

It is becoming clearer every day that the government of the *shōgun*, with whom we have made our treaties, is powerless to enforce those treaty rights. The feudal *daimyō*, with that curious personage of the emperor, are stronger than the government at Edo; and until a change takes place, resulting in the formation of a powerful government either at Kyoto or Edo, and the destruction of the feudal system, there will, I fear, be little security for the lives of our countrymen in this part of the world. How this is to be accomplished, whether by civil war or by the interference of foreign powers, is at present uncertain.

It would seem that a kind of revolution has already taken place in Edo. The *Japan Herald* of October 25th says:

> It was with no small surprise and dismay that the populace of Edo learned this week that henceforth the highest *daimyō* are only to visit Edo once in seven years, and then only for a hundred days at a time; the second class, once in three years only, and then for a hundred days; while the third are to remain as at present; but in their case, as in all the others, their wives and families are no longer to stay in Edo as hostages, but are to return and to remain in the provinces. This change, it will be seen at a glance, is a great diminution of the splendor of the *shōgun*'s position. That these highest *daimyō*, seven years hence, will think of visiting Edo for a hundred days, no one

will be simple enough to believe, or that the second class will return is exceedingly doubtful. Thus shorn of its jewels, the crown of the shogunate becomes that of head of the lower *daimyō* only. The seat of power will probably, in no long time, be removed to Kyoto.

A correspondent of *The Times* (December 29) gives another and different version of the same story:

The government of His Majesty the *shōgun* of Japan issued a notification at Edo on the 19th of October, to the effect that all *daimyō* or princes (excepting only those of the blood Royal, and also those intrusted with the direction of affairs) should respectively withdraw to their principalities,

Henceforth the government makes it no longer compulsory on them to reside at Edo; they will be called up once in three years to the metropolis for the space of a hundred days,

The Princes of Awatri, Mito, and Kishni, being of the blood Royal, they will reside at Edo by turns of one year each, one remaining while the other two are permitted to withdraw to their ancestral territories.

A further notification has been issued imposing sumptuary restrictions, and recommending economy, both in clothing and living, to the people of Japan, high and low.

A brother of the late *shōgun* has been appointed Prince Regent since the demise of the late Emperor up to the present crisis. He belonged to the priesthood, but, owing to his high consanguinity, coupled with his great talents, he has been summoned to this important post.

N.B. It is impossible to assign the true motives for such sudden and radical changes, but it does appear as though the government of the *shōgun* was much stronger than has hitherto been conceded. It is thought possible that greater liberality to foreigners may follow these events, and that a variety of restrictions hitherto imposed upon native traders may be gradually removed.

If the latter version of this strange story prove to be the correct one, better days may be in store for Japan than we had dared to hope for. It is very difficult for foreigners to understand the proceedings of this remarkable people, and future events alone can enable us to comprehend those of the present or of the past.

Farming

In the preceding chapters of this work I have noticed, from time to time, the operations of the Japanese farmer. But the agriculture of Japan is a subject of considerable interest, and worthy of more than a passing notice. In order that it may be better understood I shall first endeavour to give an account of the climate of the country.

The empire of Japan covers a space of about 15 degrees of latitude, and is placed between 30° and 45° north. It consists of four large islands, namely, Kyushu, Shikoku, Japan, and Hokkaido, and occupies a position on the eastern side of Asia not unlike that of the British Islands on the west of Europe, only considerably farther to the south. Like China it is liable to extremes of temperature—to excessive heat in summer and great cold in winter—such as are unknown on our side of the world within the same degrees of latitude. But the sea, surrounding and running between the various islands, prevents the extremes of heat and cold from being so great as they are on the mainland. Hence Japan is a much more healthy and agreeable place of residence than China, at least for the English and other inhabitants of the more temperate parts of Europe.

My remarks on climate, and the tables of temperature, &c., which I shall bring forward, apply more particularly to the island of Japan, near the capital and centre of the empire. At Nagasaki, on the island of Kyushu, in the south, the winters are less cold than at Edo; while at Hakodate, in Hokkaido, they are longer and more severe. The Russian traveller Vasily Golovnin tells us that in Hokkaido the first snow fell about the middle of October, but soon melted; winter set in about the 15th of November, with deep snow, which lasted until April. But making these allowances for the differences of latitude, the information which I shall give of the climate of Japan will present a fair idea of that of the country generally.

July and August are the two hottest months in the year, having a maximum temperature of 92 and a minimum of 63°. In January and February, the two coldest months, the temperature ranges between 18° and 69°. In some seasons it probably sinks considerably lower than it did in 1860, and no doubt it may usually be marked much lower than this in the more northern island of Hokkaido. The heat of the summer months tempered by sea breezes is easily endured, while the cold of midwinter has a bracing effect upon the constitutions of both natives and foreigners. The latter seem peculiarly healthy in Japan, and instances are not rare in which invalids from China, who have visited the country on account of their health, have been speedily cured. In March, April, and up to the middle of May (the commencement of the rains), the climate is very delightful. The autumnal months are generally of the same description; although the sun is sometimes hot in the middle of the day, yet an umbrella is not required; the air is cool and agreeable, and the evenings are most enjoyable. At this time of the year the sun, for days, and sometimes for weeks on end, rises in the morning, runs his course, and sets in the evening in a sky on which not a cloud has appeared.

The monsoons which blow steadily along the eastern coast of Asia are not so decided in their character in Japan as they are in China. Still, northerly and easterly winds prevail from September to April, and southerly and westerly during the remainder of the year. Like China this country is frequently visited by those fearful hurricanes or cyclones, commonly known as typhoons, which unroof houses, tear trees out of the ground, and wreck many a goodly vessel at sea. It is also remarkable, more than any country known to me, for the suddenness with which gales come on. The morning may be calm and beautiful, yet long before noon it may be blowing a furious gale of wind.

In Japan the rainy season is much more decided in its character than it is in China. The hearty way in which the rains come down reminded me more of the season in upper India, amongst the southern ranges of the Himalayas, than of that in China. But the rainy season in Japan is short when compared with India. It usually commences about the middle of May and lasts to the middle or end of June; and a glance at the table will show that

these two months are by far the wettest in the year. This is the time when.
the monsoon is changing from north to south. The southerly winds come
up loaded with moisture they have acquired in their passage over the sea
through warm latitudes. This moisture is suddenly condensed into thick
fogs as it comes in contact with the land, which has been cooled down to
a low temperature by the long-continued northerly winds.

In 1860 but little snow fell on the low lands, although it was plentiful
upon the adjoining mountains. But if Hepburn's table shows little snow, it
is most prolific in earthquakes. In June there were no less than eleven shocks,
and during the year the total number felt was thirty-two! When we take
into consideration the number that occurred during the hours of sleep,
which were not felt and registered, we may have some idea of the activity
of the volcanos that lie under this extraordinary country.

Having thus given some idea of the climate of Japan—of its summer and
winter, its seed time and harvest—I shall now endeavour to give a description
of its agriculture. As a profession agriculture does not hold the same rank
in Japan as it does in China. The *shōgun* does not here mark his sense of its
importance by putting his hands to the plough and throwing the first grains
of rice into the ground, as is done by the Son of Heaven. In social rank the
farmer is said to be below the Buddhist priest, the soldier, the merchant,
and even the petty shopkeeper. We are told that he is but the serf of the great
landed proprietor, and that he is heavily taxed and kept in a state of complete
degradation. I am not in a position to deny these statements, but I can affirm,
from personal observation in many parts of the country, that the farmers
and their families live in good comfortable-looking houses, are well clothed,
well fed, and appear to be happy and contented.

The geological formation of the country and the composition of the soil
vary greatly in the different districts. In the island of Kyushu, in the south,
and also in Shikoku, the upper sides of the hills are generally barren, with
rocks of clay-slate and granite protruding. On the lower sides of the hills
and in the valleys, where cultivation is carried on, the soil consists of clay
and sand mixed with vegetable matter. On the south-side of Japan, Alcock
informs us, the hills are formed of sandstone and sand, and the valleys and
plains seem little else. About three days' journey to the south of Fuji-*yama*,
the dark-rich soil of the volcanic regions first appeared. In the country

round the capital the soil is of a blackish-brown color, composed chiefly of vegetable matter, and bears some resemblance to that which is found in the peat-bogs of England. This description of soil, as I have already noticed, is not confined to the low valleys, but is also met with on the tops of the hills.

The agricultural products of Japan may be divided into two great classes, namely, the winter and the summer crops. The winter crops consist of wheat, barley, cabbage oil-plant (*Brassica sinensis*), and other cabbage for the table, together with buckwheat, peas, beans, onions, and English potatoes. The three first-mentioned may be considered as the staple winter products. All these crops are cultivated on land above the level of the rice valleys. The wheat and barley are sown in the end of October or beginning of November; these soon vegetate, and cover the hillsides with lively green during the winter months. The seed is sown in rows, about two feet three inches apart, and is dropped in the drills by the hand in patches, each containing from twenty-five to thirty seeds, these patches being about a foot apart from each other in the drill. Ab the land has been carefully cleaned and prepared previously to sowing, scarcely any farther labor is necessary during the winter and following spring.

Early in the month of April the hillsides are yellow with the flowers of the cabbage oil-plant, and the air is filled with its fragrance. About the 10th of May the wheat and barley are in full ear, and the seed-pods of the cabbage are swelling and coming fast to maturity. The latter ripens near Edo about the end of the month, and the oil harvest begins. The plant is not cut like corn, but is pulled up by the root, and laid on the field where it has been growing. When it has lain for a few days to dry, a convenient space is cleared in the middle of the prostrate crop, upon which mats are laid, and the laborers (women chiefly) take the stalks, handful by handful, and tread out the seeds upon the mats. In the beginning of June fires are seen all over the country, and smoke fills the air. The rape-seed has been harvested, and the farmers are engaged in burning the stalks and other refuse on the land, with the view of getting the ashes for the summer crops which are now being sown to take the place of the rape.

The barley harvest commences in the first days of June, and in 1861 was in full operation on the 5th of that month. The corn is cut with a small hook exactly like that used in China. A portion of this is carried home to the farmhouses at once, in order to be secure from the weather, which is rather moist at this period of the year. Here the heads of corn are separated from the stalks by beating them over a bamboo grating. The bamboo, being flinty and sharp, cuts off the heads at every stroke, and leaves them to fall through the grating to the ground. In the courtyard of every farmhouse there is a broad flooring of lime, hard and smooth, on which the corn is laid and thrashed out with a flail, in the same way as in the olden time in England.

Another portion of the crop was harvested in a most curious way, which I think must be peculiar to Japan, for I have neither seen it nor heard of it in any other country. On the 10th of June, I saw fires blazing all over the country and dense masses of smoke rising from every cornfield. This time it was not the burning of rape-stalks, for they had all disappeared, having been converted into their elements of earth and air, the former of which was already entering into another form and was supplying food for the summer crops. It was the bearded barley that was now going through the crucible, the object being to separate the heads of corn from the straw and awns. This was done in the following way—The corn, having been tied up in small bundles or sheaves, is removed to a convenient spot on the edge of the field. When the burning is to begin the workman takes a sheaf in one hand, and with the other applies fire to the upper or corn end of the sheaf. It immediately ignites, the awns go off in a blaze, the heads of corn snap from the stalk and fall to the ground. Lighting another sheaf, the workman throws the first away in a blaze, regardless apparently of the value of the straw, and so the operation goes on. As the beardless heads fall to the ground the fire goes out, leaving them slightly browned by the operation, but with the grain unharmed.

Straw is largely used for the flooring of rooms, and is laid under the matting, but, judging from the quantity burned in this way, it cannot be so valuable to the Japanese as it is to us. The object in thus burning the barley is, no doubt, to economize the space available for shelter, for, if the grain were left exposed to the rains that fall at this season, it would soon germinate and spoil. Every evening these heads of corn are packed up in baskets and carried home to the farmstead, where they are threshed out by the flail on the lime floor, as I have already described.

The wheat harvest is later than the barley, and became general about the 23rd of June. The varieties of both wheat and barley did not appear to me to be first-rate, but probably they may be more suitable to the climate of Japan than those of the higher qualities cultivated in Europe. There were two or three varieties of wheat, one of them a red kind, said to have been imported from the United States of America. By the 1st of July both barley and wheat harvests were over in Japan, and the summer crops were already progressing rapidly on what had formerly been cornfields.

The summer crops consist of two classes, one is cultivated on the dry hill or corn land, and another succeeds best in the valleys which can be irrigated. The first of these consists of soy and other beans of that class, French beans, hill rice—a kind that does not require irrigation—cotton, oily grain (*Sesamum orientale*) the eggplant, turnips, radishes, carrots, onions, *gobō* (*Arctium gobbo*), or burdock, cucumbers and melons, ginger yams, and sweet potatoes.

No time is lost in getting these crops into the ground. The corn, I have already observed, is grown in rows, and some time before it is ripe the spaces between the rows are carefully weeded, stirred up, and manured with burnt ashes. The summer crops are then sown or planted between the rows of the ripening corn, and have made considerable progress in their growth before it is harvested. In this way a longer season of growth is secured. When the corn has been cut, the stubble, after a short time, is hoed up and drawn to the side of the new crop, where it rots and forms manure.

The manures that are used for these crops consist chiefly of burnt ashes at the time of sowing, and of night-soil diluted with water during the period of growth. Night-soil and urine are carefully collected and deposited in large earthen jars, which are sunk on the sides of the fields.

Sweet potatoes are preserved during winter in a square plot of ground in the farmyard. This is surrounded with a straw fence, and covered over with paddy husks and straw when the weather is cold. Early in May—the winter covering having been removed—the potatoes begin to grow rapidly, and send out numerous young shoots, which are made into cuttings, and transplanted at once into the fields. This transplanting commences about the end of May, and continues all June. When these cuttings are put into the ground, they seem to form roots and grow as easily as couch grass. But then this operation takes place during the rainy season, when the sky is often cloudy, and when the air is charged with moisture—a circumstance that fully accounts for its success.

The second class of summer crops are those that grow chiefly in the low valleys, and require irrigation during the period of their growth. Rice, the staple food of the people, is one of the principal of these, and by far the most important. The variety in cultivation is, I think, superior to the kinds met with in China and in India, and is probably the best in Asia.

The rice-lands generally lie fallow all the winter, and consequently yield only one crop in the year. In the last days of April, or about the first of May, little patches of land are prepared in the comers of the fields as seed-beds for the young paddy. Here the seed is sown thickly, sometimes having been steeped in liquid manure previously to its being sown. It vegetates in a wonderfully short space of time—three or four days, if the weather be warm and moist, as it generally is at this season of the year. In the mean time, while this is vegetating in the seed beds, the laborers are busily employed in preparing the land into which it is to be transplanted.

In China the rice-land is usually prepared by the plough and harrow, drawn by the bullock or the buffalo. These animals are rarely seen in Japan employed in this way; at least, they did not come under my observation. The rice-lands are prepared almost entirely by manual labor, A strong three-pronged fork, having the prongs bent like a hoe, is used for this purpose. The land is then flooded, and manured with grass and weeds cut and brought from adjacent waste ground, and used in a fresh state as I have already described. The surface of the fields is then made smooth, and is considered ready for the young rice in the seed beds.

The transplanting of the young paddy commences about the 8th of June. About three inches of water cover the surface of the fields, and the planting goes on with the most astonishing rapidity. The work is performed exactly in the same way as it is in China. A laborer takes a load of plants under his left arm, and drops them in little bundles over the surface of the land about to be planted, knowing, almost to a plant, what number will be required. Others, both men and women, take up the bundles thus thrown down, and the planting commences. The proper number of plants are selected and planted in rows, by hand, in the muddy soil. When the hand is drawn up, the water rushes in, carrying down with it a portion of the soil, and thus the roots are covered instantaneously. Cranes, or herons, follow the laborers in the fields, and pick up the worms. The planting season is at its height about the 21st of June, and is generally over by the 10th of July. On some lands the seed is sown thinly, broadcast, and here, of course, no transplanting is necessary; this sowing takes place from the 15th to the 20th of May.

As the rice valleys near Kanagawa are intersected and surrounded by hills from which streams of water are continually flowing, it is not necessary to irrigate the fields by waterwheels, as in China. The streams are led, in the first place, into the fields near the foot of the hills, where the land is highest. Little ridges of earth or grassy embankments surround the different fields, each having a small space for the ingress and egress of the water. In this manner the hill stream first floods one field to the desired depth, then flows into the next at the point of egress, and so on, until the whole valley is irrigated. Natural or artificial watercourses, with channels lower than the fields, run through these rice valleys, and when the water is no longer required it is led into these, and carried out to the sea. By this means the water is kept always under the most perfect control; and in the autumn, when the ripening crops no longer require its aid, the little points of ingress are closed up, and the stream is allowed to flow in its natural channel.

During the remainder of the summer and autumn the paddy requires little more than attention to the irrigation, and now and then loosening and stirring up the soil between the rows, and removing any weeds. It is ripe and is harvested in November.

Amongst other agricultural products that grow in the valleys of Japan, may be mentioned the eatable arum (*Arum esculentum*), the water chestnut (*Scirpus tuberosus*), and the soft rush (*Juncus effusus*), the latter being used in the manufacture of the *tatami* mats so common in the country. In the lakes and ponds large quantities of nelumbium roots are grown, and are used as a vegetable and also in the production of a kind of arrowroot.

Such is a short account of Japanese farming as it presented itself to me in the autumn and winter of 1860, and spring and summer of 1861. The farms are small in extent when compared with those in western countries, and the homesteads also present a very different appearance to ours. They have no lowing of oxen or bleating of sheep; a stray packhorse or a solitary ox may sometimes be seen, but these are only used as beasts of burden. Pigs may sometimes be seen, but they are generally kept in the background out of view; even though pork is abundant in the butchers' shops. Goats and sheep do not appear to be indigenous; some of the latter have been imported from China, but the experiment of acclimatizing them has not yet succeeded. They invariably become diseased, and die off. Cows or oxen are little used in agriculture, and it is probable that the Japanese, like their neighbours in China, have religious scruples as to using such animals for food.

It has been frequently repeated, by writers on Japan, that hardly a foot of ground, to the very tops of the mountains, is left uncultivated. I have already shown in a previous chapter that such is not the case; that thousands of acres of fertile land are lying uncultivated, and covered with trees planted by nature, and brushwood, of little value. One naturally asks why these lands, which are capable of cultivation, should be allowed to lie in this unproductive condition. Is it because there is more than enough to supply the wants of a people that, for ages past, have been shut out from the rest of the world, and have therefore, while they have not contributed to the wants of others, been accustomed to rely entirely upon themselves for food and clothing?

I cannot conclude this description of Japanese agriculture without noticing the remarkable connection that exists between the climate and the products of the country, and how well they are suited to each other. The rainy season does not come on until the dry winter and spring crops are ripe, and ready to be harvested. When the rice-planting begins, and when the cuttings of the sweet potato are being put out, the air becomes loaded with moisture, and the rain comes down in torrents. Every hill stream is filled with water, and thus the means of irrigating the ricefields are ready to the hands of the farmer. Such excessive moisture would have been fatal to the wheat and barley and rape, but it gives life and vigor to the paddy and sweet potatoes, and is necessary for their health and luxuriance. The tea-plant, too, which, at this season, has had its first leaves plucked, is revived by the moist air and frequent showers, and is enabled to push forth with renewed vigor, and to yield fresh supplies. And when excessive moisture is no longer necessary to these summer products, the rain ceases, the sky becomes clear, and the air comparatively dry. Then the process of ripening begins, and a sunny autumn enables the farmer to gather into his bars the fruits of his anxious labors.

Silk and Tea

In addition to the agricultural products I have just described, there are many other articles in the country pleasant to the sight and good for food, which are worthy of attention now that the Japanese have entered into the great family of nations. Perhaps no country in the world is more independent of other countries than Japan. She has, within herself, enough to supply all the wants and luxuries of life. The products of the tropics, as well as those of temperate regions, are found in her fields and gathered into her barns. Wherever there are mountain ranges, coal, lead, iron, and copper are found, and not unfrequently the precious metals. Tea, silk, cotton, vegetable wax, and oils are produced in abundance all over the country. Ginseng and other medicines, with salt fish and seaweed, are largely exported to China.

Silk and tea are, at present, the most important and valuable articles of export to Europe and America. I am indebted to William Keswick, of the well-known house of Jardine, Matheson, and Co., one of the earliest settlers at Yokohama, for the following information regarding these articles of export. As Keswick was daily in communication with merchants from all parts of the country, and as he had considerable knowledge of the language, his means of acquiring information of this kind were greatly superior to my own:

> Silk is more or less produced in almost every province of the island of Japan north of Osaka, but the four districts in which it is found in the greatest abundance are Ōshū (Mutsu), Jōshū (Hitachi), Kōshū (Kai), and Shinshū (Shinano). Ōshū produces the largest quantity, but the silk does not equal in quality and fineness of size that of the

other districts. Jōshū and Shinshū are noted for the fine size of their
silk; and even in the London market, when the best China silk was
selling at 25., it brought as high a price as 305. per lb.

These districts are situated in the northern part of the island of Japan,
and I believe are nearer to the port of Hakodate than to Yokohama. Japanese
silk is more carefully reeled than Chinese, and is generally of better quality.
At present it is nearly all bought for the continent, and much more would
be consumed if it could be obtained.

Tea is produced, or grows wild, in all the provinces of the island of
Kyushu, and throughout the greater part of Japan. The finest qualities
come from Yamashiro, but the two largest producing districts are Ise
and Owari. Suruga, Shimōsa, and Kai are the provinces that supply the
Kanagawa market with the earliest new tea; but as the season advances,
large supplies arrive from the provinces bordering on the Inland Sea.

The tea plant is said to have been introduced into Japan from China about
the beginning of the ninth century by a Buddhist priest named Saichō, who
presented the first cup of the beverage to the reigning emperor. It is now
constantly observed on the sides of the roads, and in the gardens of the
farmers and cottagers, who appear in many instances to cultivate only as
much as will supply the wants of their families. I met with it in this way
about Nagasaki and Kanagawa, and in larger quantities in the vicinity of the
capital. There can be no doubt, I think, that the great tea districts of Japan
are near Osaka and Kyoto, the residence of the emperor. Should this prove
correct, then the new port of Hyōgo, in the Inland Sea, or some place in
its vicinity, may, one day, prove of considerable value to our merchants.

Curious and almost romantic statements have been published regarding
the mode of cultivating the tea-plant in Japan—statements that, I am afraid,
are more carious than truthful. Take the following as an example:

The plantations are situated remote from the habitations of man, and
as much as may be from all other crops, lest the delicacy of the tea
should suffer from smoke, impurity, or contamination of any kind.

They are manured with dried anchovies and a liquor pressed out of mustard seed. They must enjoy the unobstructed beams of the morning sun, and thrive best upon well-watered hillsides. The plant is pollarded to render it more branching, and therefore more productive, and must be five years old before the leaves are gathered.

(!) How our worthy tea-farmers in Japan and China would laugh if they were told that such things were written about their mode of cultivating the tea plant!

Such statements remind me of reading, in a book on China, an account of rice cultivation, in which the writer cannot understand the practice of sowing the rice-seeds very thickly in highly manured beds in the corners of the fields. He sagely concludes that it must be upon the principle of "the more the merrier"! It never occurred to his mind that these are merely seedbeds, where the plants are being reared for the purpose of transplanting, and that he may see the same kind of practice in any cabbage garden in England. And the readers of the remarks on tea cultivation quoted above may rest assured that this useful plant may be cultivated successfully, although not remote from the habitations of man, or manured with dried anchovies and mustard seed oil. I may perhaps be pardoned for referring those interested in the matter to my *Three Years' Wanderings in China* and *Journey to the Tea Countries* where the cultivation and manufacture of tea, have been fully described from personal observation.

From a return made out by Consul Vyse and presented to Parliament, it appears that the value of the raw silk and silk manufactures exported from Kanagawa during the year ending the 31st December, 1860, was 548,630*l*. 13*s*. 4*d*. The value of tea exported during the same period was 64,260*l*. 16*s*. 8*d*. The total value of the exports from this port in 1860 amounted to 865,200*l*., the principal articles besides silk and tea being copper, oil, and seeds, dried fish, seaweed, medicine, vegetable wax, and lacquerware.

One of the merchants, in a letter to H. B. Majesty's Consul, dated August 8th, 1861, remarks:

In point of value the business transacted at this port during the first six months of 1861 far exceeds what was transacted during the same period of 1860… To show you that there has been a rapid development of the export trade, I need only state that from July, 1859, to July, 1860, the export of silk was about 5000 bales; from July, 1860, to July, 1861, it was 12,000 bales. Of tea, from July, 1859, to July, 1860, there are no statistics, but the export was a mere trifle; whereas, from July, 1860, to July, 1861, it amounted to near 6,000,000 lbs. Such figures as these place the growing nature of our trade, and its importance, beyond question, and require no comment.

From my own observations in different parts of the country, I am fully convinced that the Japanese have the means of producing an almost unlimited supply of both these staple articles of export, and more particularly of tea. Thousands of acres of valuable land, on which the tea plant would yield an abundant crop of leaves, are now lying waste, or in an unproductive condition. We may, therefore, look forward with confidence to increased supplies of tea from Japan, and also, I hope, to an improvement in their manipulation, and consequently in their flavor.

When the other ports and cities named in the treaty are opened to foreign trade, there will be a large increase in the value of both exports and imports. But the Japanese authorities are making great exertions to put off, what appears to them to be, "the evil day." The *shōgun* himself has written a letter to Her Majesty the Queen of Great Britain, in which he states, "there are various objections that the Article of the treaty providing for the opening of the ports of Hyōgo and Niigata, and for the carrying on of trade in the cities of Edo and Osaka, should be brought into operation on the conditions stated therein;" and he desires, therefore, "to defer the opening of these places for a time." The ministers for foreign affairs, also, have addressed Alcock upon the same subject. They begin by stating that nearly three hundred years have elapsed since the empire discontinued its intercourse with foreign powers; that recently, in consequence of the urgent advice of the president of the United States and of the king of the Netherlands, this old-standing law was altered, and foreign vessels, sailing near the coasts, were allowed to put in at the ports of Shimoda and Hakodate for fuel, provisions, and water.

Again, after the arrival of the American minister, the government, having taken into consideration the existing posture of foreign affairs, concluded the treaty of amity that lately entered into operation, and established free trade in the same manner, first with Great Britain, &c. But the actual result of this proceeding differed considerably from what had been anticipated. No profit has yet been derived; but the lower classes of the people have already suffered loss thereby. The price of things is daily increasing, in consequence of the large quantity of products that are exported to foreign countries; and the people, when deprived of the means of gaining their livelihood, ascribe the cause to trade and are discontented. Even the wealthier classes, it is hinted, are likely to condemn the abrogation of the previously existing prohibition, and may desire the restitution of the former law. This being the result of opening two or three ports to foreign trade, everyone is grieved when he reads the stipulations of the treaty, which state that the ports of Hyōgo and Niigata are to be opened, and that foreign trade will also be carried on at the cities of Edo and Osaka, by which the loss and the injury will be still further increased.

The ministers further state that "the popular spirit having already arrived at such a pitch, it is very difficult even for the power and the authority of the government so to manage that each one should clearly understand the future advantage, and to cause them to endure for a time the present grief." Should the government use violence in carrying out the stipulations of the treaty, "it would be uncertain what mischief would result from such an act against the national spirit."

In order, therefore, not to press too heavily upon the people, and to give time to the ignorant to accustom themselves to free trade, and to feel its benefits, the ministers propose to defer the opening of the two ports and two cities for the space of seven years, and to agree that they shall be opened in 1868.

The document, of which I have just given the substance, is an able one, and demands most careful attention from the governments of foreign powers who have treaties with Japan. As a general rule it is bad policy to waive any treaty right with Orientals, as, in the case of China and the question of our being allowed to enter the city of Canton, such a proceeding may plunge us into future and expensive wars. But the Japanese question is a peculiar one. The government evidently felt it had committed a mistake when it agreed to the treaty, and would now gladly return to the old state of things.

As its experience of foreigners had been confined to the Dutch at Deshima, who had carried on their trade in one or two ships a year, it had no idea that merchants with large capitals would come in such numbers, and that fleets of ships would arrive to carry off the produce of the country. And the statements the ministers now made were perfectly true; provisions had increased in price; the people were getting discontented, attributing the rise in prices to the presence and action of foreigners, and not understanding or caring for free-trade and its future benefits. In this state of things it is not at all unlikely that, if the opening of the new ports were pressed, a rebellion might take place which the government would not have the power to put down.

There may be a difference of opinion as to the propriety of agreeing to defer the opening of Hyōgo and Osaka, with another port on the west coast instead of Niigata, but, I think, all who have studied the matter must agree as to the necessity of not pressing, at present at least, the opening of Edo. I believe, even if it were agreed to by the government, it would be attended with the greatest danger. I have already shown the character of the population that crowds the streets of this city—idle retainers from all parts of the country, full of prejudice against foreigners, always armed with sharp swords, and ready to use them on the slightest provocation, or with no provocation at all. Against these men and their masters the government itself would seem to be almost powerless. "Both the American treaties were inaugurated by the death of the reigning *shōgun* who signed or sanctioned them, the first by the sword and the second by poison. One of the royal brothers was deposed and exiled, and the regent of the kingdom was slain in revenge for this act by the *daimyō* of Mito's followers"(Alcock's despatch to Earl Russell).

A city like this would, therefore, be a most unsafe place for a number of foreigners, full of life and high spirits, with customs and manners very different from those of the Japanese, and which the latter, oftentimes, can neither understand nor appreciate. In such a place life and property would always be insecure, and it is not unlikely that, sooner or later, a general massacre might be attempted. With these things before our eyes—believing the government to be anxious for our safety, but to be almost powerless, feeling its weakness and dreading the future, are we prepared to incur the risk of opening Edo, or to punish the government if it fails to protect us? It seems idle to talk of holding the government responsible for our safety in a country where it is so weak as not to be able to protect itself. Taking, therefore, into consideration the dangers attending the opening of Edo to foreign merchants, and the fact that we have already a port of trade within a few miles of it to which its produce can be easily brought, where we can reside and trade in comparative security, I think it will be wise to waive our right to the opening of that city, at least for the present.

It seems doubtful whether we should also give way to the proposal of deferring the opening of Hyōgo and Osaka, in the Inland Sea, as also of a port on the west coast, should a suitable one be found there, to take the place of Niigata. Although the ignorance and prejudices of the people may be as great against us in these places as at Edo, yet the same dangers to life and property are certainly not so apparent. And if it be worth our while to have a footing in these places at all, it is almost certain that the difficulties in our way will be as great seven years hence as they are at the present time. We might, therefore, meet the Japanese government half-way, by insisting that the provisions of the treaty be carried out in so far as these places are concerned, while we waived, for the present, our right of residing and trading in the capital itself.

But it seems doubtful whether the *shōgun*'s government has the power to ratify the treaties made with foreign nations without the sanction of the emperor; and this high and mysterious personage, it is suspected, has not yet given such sanction. The following note on this subject has just appeared in the *China Mail*, and is worth attentive perusal:

> It is well known now that the emperor has not yet given his formal consent to the treaties made with the foreign powers, and it must be evident that without his consent those treaties have no legal value in the eyes of the Japanese *daimyō* and people. This, then, is the root of all the recent troubles. This is the reason why the *shōgun*'s government is not able to defend our ministers and us, and is hardly able to defend itself, from the attacks of the malcontents who seek its embarrassment or our expulsion. This is why it does not and dare not punish those assassins who from time to time cut unoffending

foreigners to pies in the open streets, or in the very teeth of the native guard and at the door of the British minister. This is why it endeavours to restrict our trade and to make its further pursuit uninviting, this is why it refused to open Edo last January, and is reluctant to open Osaka next January. This is why we are desired to retire to Nagasaki, where foreign trade has long been established, and are offered there the facilties denied us here (Edo). In short, this is why there is no peace or friendship for foreigners in this part of Japan, and why neither our political nor our commercial relations with this people are what they ought to be. It is not pretended that the *shōgun*'s government is implicated in the numerous crimes which have marked with tracks of blood the history of our three years' relations with Japan. Doubtless this government deplores those crimes as sincerely as anyone. But it is powerless to prevent them; and for this plain reason—that it has not yet been able to abolish one of the laws of Gongen-*sama* [Tokugawa Ieyasu], in virtue of which licence is given to slay foreigners wherever they may be found. It is, then, useless for us to wait here with our lives in our hands while the *shōgun* slowly gathers from our trade, and from his own enterprises, the means and the power to overcome these laws, and to redeem his promises to us. Either we must leave the country, or we must obtain from the only ruler who is supreme in it the full rat-ification of the rights and privileges we came here to enjoy. There is no middle course. Compromises, postponements, concessions, all half-measures, are of no avail in this matter. I repeat, therefore, that the alternative is either to have the treaties recognized by the real government of the empire, or to abandon them as worthless, and depart from a country where we are unwelcome and unsafe.

As a place of trade, Japan, with all its advantages, has been probably overrated, particularly as a market for our manufactures. There is no doubt, however, that it can supply us with large quantities of silk and tea, and thus render us less dependent on China for those articles that have now become indispensable to our happiness and comfort. But as a customer to our manu-facturing districts, Japan will never be equal to China.

As merchants, too, the Chinese appear to be far ahead of the Japanese. While a Japanese wonld be haggling for a few cash on a hank of silk or a pound of tea, a Chinaman would be quietly settling for a shipload of the same articles. Experience has also shown that the Chinese trader is more to be depended on than the Japanese. Indeed, as merchants of honor and talent I doubt if the former are to be excelled in any part of the world. That pithy little sentence which concludes a bargain, "put-e-book," or "book it," is considered as binding as if it was registered by the Bank of England; and rarely indeed will a Chinaman recede from his bargain, even if its fulfilment should involve him in an unfortunate speculation. At present this cannot be said of the Japanese; but they may probably improve when they become better acquainted with foreigners, and when others, now in the background, come into the field.

Traders in Japan, however wealthy or intelligent, are looked down upon with disdain by the merest serf of the *daimyō*; and the merchants of foreign countries are treated much in the same way. This state of things will not surprise anyone acquainted with the history of our own country in the feudal ages.

It is to be feared that foreign officials, desirous of not being confounded with the inferior orders of their countrymen, do not contribute in any way to lessen this feeling, but, on the contrary, oftentimes give it a kind of official sanction. This is unfortunate, but I fear it is too true. It will scarcely be credited in a country like England, where our merchants and sons of merchants occupy some of the highest positions in the kingdom, and where anyone who took it into his head to act in such a manner would only be laughed at for his pains. But things are done in a different way in Japan.

With all our care in opening up this trade, it is much to be feared that a time may come—and that it is not very distant—when Japan will have to pay dearly for her former exclusive policy. As a nation we have an abhorrence of war and all its attendant horrors, but somehow or other— owing, no doubt, partly to our wide-spread dominions and to our extensive commerce—we have war always forced upon us against our inclinations; and that this will be one of the results of our new treaty with Japan, there is, as I have already said, but too much reason to anticipate.

Departure

Having thus endeavored to give some description of the climate, agriculture, products, and trade of Japan, I shall now resume my narrative.

It was now the middle of July, the rains were over for the season, and the days were sometimes oppressively hot. The thermometer ranged from 80° to 90° Fahrenheit. The foreign community were still in a high state of excitement, and rumors of fresh attacks from some source—no one knew from where—were freely circulated in yokohama and Kanagawa. Jan Karel de Wit, the minister of the Netherlands, was residing in the house of his consul at Yokohama, and had a guard of men from a ship of war then in the harbour. One morning we were told that an attack had been made on his house during the night by an armed band, who, luckily for him, had been observed and beaten off by the guard. De Wit had been one of the party who had come overland from Nagasaki with Alcock, and it was alleged that his life was sought for on that account. Another report stated that there had been no attack at all, but that the guard had been indulging rather freely in strong drinks, by which means it had been enabled to see an attacking force which existed only in an overheated imagination. Then another Dutchman, who was sleeping at the hotel of the town, was alarmed by a two-sworded man entering his bedroom in the dead of the night, in search, it was supposed, of the correspondent of the *Illustrated London News*, then staying at the hotel, who had also been another of the offending overland party. The good Dutchman was greatly alarmed, and did not appreciate the honor of being killed in the place of "Our own Correspondent." There were sceptics amongst us who did not credit these rumors, and I merely mention them to show the state of alarm which then existed.

At this time I was still living alone in my large temple at Kanagawa. One day, as I was sitting in the verandah arranging my herbarium and drying my paper, several two-sworded men made their appearance at the end of the avenue. I began to speculate on the chance of an attack, when I was relieved from all apprehension by seeing a number of others come upon the scene, amongst whom there appeared to be some persons of high rank. An interpreter was sent forward to inform me that the governor himself was my visitor, and that he had come to make an inspection of the paling and hedges which surrounded the grounds, in order to see whether there were any holes through which *rōnin* could crawl and do me mortal injury. If any such holes existed, he was good enough to say, he would have them repaired. The idea was an amusing one, and calculated to excite a smile on my countenance. If any *rōnin* wanted me, they could have had no difficulty in getting in even after the fence was repaired; but being in Japan, I took the matter very gravely, and asked the interpreter to express my thanks to his Excellency the governor for his care for my safety.

The governor and his attendants now made the circuit of the fences, and examined all the weak places, after which they returned to me on the verandah of the temple. It was now explained to me that one or two little holes existed which should be closed, and that the gate of the cemetery which led into the ground would be nailed up. I was then asked to what nation I belonged—was I English, French, or American? I replied I was an Englishman. Was I a government official or a merchant? I was neither, but had visited Japan for the purpose of making collections of natural history. I then showed them my stores of living and dried plants, insects, shells, and books, with which they appeared greatly pleased. I explained to them that in England we had such things introduced from all parts of the world, and that I was now endeavoring to add to our collections all that was useful or beautiful in Japan. They understood and apparently appreciated my objects, and mentioned that they knew Von Siebold, who was engaged in similar pursuits. When my collections had been inspected, the governor inquired if I was living alone in the temple, and seemed to be surprised when he was informed that no one was with me except my servants. I then desired the linguist to ask him if he thought there was any danger to be apprehended, and had the following consolatory and cautious reply—"The governor cannot say there is no danger, but he will see that the fences are repaired." This remark was followed by a polite "goodbye" as the party took their leave, and left me alone to my meditations.

All was now bustle and excitement in Kanagawa, and the carpenters in particular appeared to be driving a brisk trade. The fences of the different consulates, and those of the few unofficial foreign residents, were repaired, some of them being doubled, heightened, and armed with spikes and nails. Guards were stationed both in the front and in the rear of the different houses, and the government appeared to be taking every means in its power for our safety. I believed then, and it is my opinion still, that the Japanese were acting in good faith, and that they were really doing everything in their power, in their own way, to protect us from the vengeance of the dreaded *rōnin*.

This state of things was exciting enough, but I must confess that it was far from being agreeable. I did not care much for any attack that might be made upon us during the day-time, when one would have an opportunity of either fighting or running away; but the prospect of being murdered in bed, while one slept, was quite another thing; and as I was alone in a large rambling building, I might have fallen an easy victim during the night, without anyone being aware of it until the following day. In these circumstances, going to bed at night was about the most unpleasant part of the day's operations. My work, however, was nearly finished; and after a few days of this excitement I was able to go over to Yokohama, where the principal portion of the foreign community resided. Here I was kindly received by William Gregson Aspinall, a gentleman whom I had formerly known in China, and who had established a firm in Japan.

It was now the end of July, and a great change had taken place in the appearance of the flora of the country. Flowers had nearly disappeared in the vegetation. With the exception of Hydrangeas, Hollyhocks, Hibiscus, and some few weeds on the roadsides, there was now nothing in bloom. The common Hydrangea grows to a great size in Japan, and forms a most remarkable and beautiful object when in flower.

I had now accomplished the object I had in view in coming to Zipangu. I had carefully examined the country during autumn and winter, spring and summer, in search of new trees and other plants of an ornamental character likely to prove suitable to our English climate. Large collections of insects and land shells had also been made; and my spare time had been employed in procuring examples of works of art, particularly of ancient lacquer, for which this country has long been famous in Europe. The agriculture of Japan—the products of the hills and those of the plains, the wet crops and the dry ones—had been carefully examined at the different seasons, and fully described from time to time in my journal. While engaged in work of this kind I came much in contact with various classes of the people, and had an opportunity of observing their habits and customs in daily life. The political state of the country, its relations with foreign powers, and the prospects of foreign trade, had all passed in review before me, and enabled me to draw my own conclusions. This was the work I had proposed to myself to do, and thus far it had been brought to a successful termination.

My collections of living plants and other objects of natural history were now very large and valuable, and the whole had to be arranged and packed. I decided to take them over to China under my own care, as the monsoon was still blowing strong from the south, and it was too early to ship them for home. A number of Ward's cases made for me by Japanese carpenters were now filled with soil, and planted with many rare and beautiful examples of the trees and shrubs of Japan. During the operation of planting I was visited by many of the inhabitants of Kanagawa, who evidently watched my proceedings with a good deal of curiosity and interest. They had never seen such queer little greenhouses before, and made many inquiries regarding the treatment of the plants during their long voyage. When I told them that the plants would be four or five months at sea, and that during that long period they would never receive any water—that in fact the cases would never be opened from the time they left China until they reached England—they looked rather puzzled and incredulous; but this was not to be wondered at, as that little fact has puzzled wiser heads than theirs.

When I had got everything ready for shipment, Her Majesty's consul, Captain Howard Vyse, to whom I was indebted for many acts of courtesy during my residence in Kanagawa, gave me a note to the customhouse authorities, who allowed me to ship my collections free of duty, and, what was of even more importance, without being opened and unpacked.

On the morning of the 29th of July, 1861, the *Fiery Cross*, Captain Crockett, in which I was a passenger, got her steam up and stood out to sea. As we passed rapidly onwards towards the mouth of the bay, the towns of Yokohama and Kanagawa, with the well-known headlands in their vicinity, gradually disappeared from our view, and I bade farewell to the green hills and lovely scenery of Japan.

bettō:	Footman.
bikuni:	Mid-Edo period prostitute who dressed to resemble Buddhist nuns and chanted the *nenbutsu* to attract customers.
bonsai:	Art form using cultivation techniques to produce small trees that mimic the shape and scale of full size trees.
chonmage:	Topknot.
daimyō:	Feudal lord.
harakiri:	Disembowelment.
hifune:	Lit. "fire ship," i.e., denoting a steamship.
ichibu:	Square silver plate Tokugawa currency. One *ōban* was equivalent to a quarter *ryō*.
jinja:	Shrine.
kago:	Palanquin.
kamon:	Family crest.
mase:	Edo slang for silver coin, and meaning "cupellated silver."
metsuke:	Inspector.
mikado:	Emperor.
nada:	Open sea.
norimono:	Carriage.
ri:	3.9 km.
rōnin:	Masterless samurai.
sake:	Japanese rice wine.
shima:	Island.

shōgun:	Hereditary military ruler during Japan's feudal era.
tairō:	Chief minister of the Tokugawa shogunate.
tatami:	Straw mat roughly six by three feet.
tempo:	Referring either to silver of gold coinage from the Tempo era.
tōjin:	Chinese or foreigner.
torii:	Gateway built at the entrance to a Shintō shrine.
uguisu:	Bush warbler (*Horornis diphone*).
yakunin:	Official.
yama:	Mountain.
yamabushi:	Reclusive mountain monks of the Japanese Alps, who practiced austerities in the harsh environment of the mountains in order to attain superhuman powers.

Index

TOYO PRess: Explore Dream Discover

Editorial supervision: William de Lange. Book and cover design: Chōkei Studios. Printing and binding: IngramSpark. The typefaces used are Perpetua, Prescript, and Herculanum.

www.ingramcontent.com/pod-product-compliance
Lightning Source LLC
Chambersburg PA
CBHW061446150726
47987CB00001B/349